AVERY LOCKE

Python Serverless Framework For Beginners

*This book was professionally typeset on Reedsy.
Find out more at reedsy.com*

Contents

Introduction: The Rise of Serverless Architecture and Why Python is Perfect for It

What is Serverless Computing?

Serverless computing represents a fundamental shift in how we build, deploy, and manage applications. It eliminates the need to manage the underlying infrastructure, such as servers, virtual machines, or containers, while allowing developers to focus solely on writing code. The term "serverless" can be somewhat misleading; servers still exist, but they are managed entirely by the cloud provider. This approach abstracts away the traditional infrastructure, relieving developers from tasks like server provisioning, scaling, and maintenance.

Instead of dealing with complex server management, in a serverless architecture, developers define small, independent functions or services that run in response to events. These functions are ephemeral, meaning they only run when needed, and scale automatically based on demand. When the function is idle, no resources are consumed, which is one of the reasons why serverless architectures can be incredibly cost-efficient.

The core concept of serverless revolves around Functions as a Service (FaaS), where developers write discrete functions that execute in response to triggers, such as an API call, file upload, or database change. Amazon Web Services (AWS) Lambda, Google Cloud Functions, and Microsoft Azure Functions are some of the most popular serverless platforms.

In a traditional architecture, developers often have to worry about over-provisioning or under-provisioning resources. If you expect a surge in traffic, you might provision more servers or increase instance sizes to handle the load. However, if traffic doesn't spike, those extra resources go to waste. Conversely, under-provisioning can result in application downtime and a poor user experience. Serverless solves this issue by dynamically scaling resources based on the actual demand. When traffic spikes, the cloud provider automatically allocates more resources, and when traffic decreases, resources are reduced, ensuring you only pay for what you use.

In a serverless environment, several components work together seamlessly:

- **Event Sources:** Events like HTTP requests, file uploads, or database updates trigger the functions.
- **Functions:** These are stateless, modular pieces of code that execute based on events.
- **Managed Services:** Cloud providers offer managed services like databases, file storage, and monitoring to integrate with serverless functions.

By embracing serverless computing, businesses can launch applications faster, without being bogged down by infrastructure concerns. Developers get to focus on writing business logic rather than managing servers, leading to quicker iterations and a faster time-to-market.

Why Choose Python for Serverless?

Python's popularity has surged across multiple domains, from web development to data science, machine learning, and automation. The rise of serverless computing is another domain where Python shines, due to its versatility, ease of use, and robust ecosystem. But why is Python particularly well-suited for serverless computing?

1. Easy-to-Learn Syntax

Python is known for its simple and readable syntax. For developers building serverless applications, this means they can write concise, clear code without the need for verbose constructs. Its simplicity allows even beginners to quickly pick up the language and start deploying serverless functions.

2. Rich Ecosystem and Libraries

Python boasts an extensive ecosystem of libraries and frameworks, making it ideal for serverless development. Whether you're building APIs, working with data, or creating web services, Python has a library for it. Libraries like **Flask** and **FastAPI** enable rapid API development, while **Boto3** provides seamless interaction with AWS services like Lambda, S3, and DynamoDB.

This wide array of libraries significantly accelerates development, as you can leverage pre-built tools and frameworks to solve common problems. In serverless, where efficiency is key, Python's ecosystem ensures that you can integrate with cloud services effortlessly and develop sophisticated applications faster.

3. Great for Prototyping and Experimentation

Because of its dynamic nature and ease of use, Python is ideal for rapid prototyping. You can experiment with ideas, test different approaches, and deploy serverless functions without getting bogged down in boilerplate code. This flexibility allows developers to iterate quickly and bring features to production faster, which is crucial for startups and fast-paced environments.

4. Compatibility with Major Cloud Providers

Python is natively supported by major serverless platforms, including AWS Lambda, Google Cloud Functions, and Microsoft Azure Functions. The ability to seamlessly deploy Python code across multiple platforms makes it an attractive option for developers who need portability and flexibility in their applications.

Moreover, AWS Lambda, one of the most popular serverless platforms, has excellent support for Python, including integrations with AWS services like DynamoDB, S3, and API Gateway. Python developers can easily interact with these services using the **Boto3** SDK, which simplifies the integration of Python functions with the AWS ecosystem.

5. Excellent for Event-Driven Programming

In a serverless architecture, applications are often event-driven. Python's asynchronous programming capabilities, particularly with libraries like **asyncio** and **AioHTTP**, make it highly efficient at handling events and I/O-bound tasks. You can create functions that respond to external events (like HTTP requests or file uploads) efficiently, without blocking other operations, which is essential for high-performance serverless applications.

6. Cost-Efficiency

Serverless computing is inherently cost-efficient because you only pay for the execution time of your functions. Python, being a high-level, interpreted language, tends to have relatively fast execution times, especially when compared to languages like Java or C#. This makes Python an excellent choice for minimizing the costs of running serverless functions, particularly when you're billed based on execution duration.

7. Community Support and Documentation

Python has one of the largest and most active developer communities in the world. This means there are abundant resources, tutorials, and documentation available, making it easier to learn, troubleshoot, and implement serverless solutions. Whether you're a beginner looking to learn Python or a seasoned developer seeking advanced techniques, you'll find plenty of support within the Python community.

8. Machine Learning and Data Processing Capabilities

Python's dominance in the data science and machine learning domains also makes it an ideal choice for serverless architectures that need to handle data-heavy or machine learning workloads. With libraries like **NumPy**, **Pandas**, **TensorFlow**, and **Scikit-learn**, you can build serverless applications that process and analyze large datasets or deploy machine learning models on the fly.

For instance, you could create a serverless function that processes incoming data streams, analyzes the data using machine learning models, and triggers further actions based on the results — all within a Python-based serverless architecture.

Benefits of Serverless Architectures (Scalability, Cost-efficiency, Performance)

Now that we've established why Python is an ideal language for serverless, it's important to understand the broader benefits of serverless computing, which have fueled its rapid adoption.

1. Scalability

One of the most attractive features of serverless computing is its ability to scale automatically. Traditionally, scaling applications required manually adding or removing servers, configuring load balancers, and handling the underlying infrastructure. In a serverless environment, scaling is fully automated. The cloud provider dynamically adjusts the resources needed based on traffic and demand, whether you're handling a few requests or millions.

When a function is invoked, the cloud provider handles the scaling for you. If there's a spike in traffic, the system automatically provisions more compute resources to handle the load. When demand decreases, the system scales back, ensuring that you're not paying for idle resources.

This seamless scalability is particularly useful for unpredictable workloads, such as handling API requests during peak traffic, or event-driven workflows that experience bursts of activity. Developers no longer have to worry about provisioning too many or too few resources, as the platform scales functions in real-time to meet demand.

2. Cost-efficiency

Serverless computing follows a "pay-as-you-go" model, meaning you only pay for the compute time consumed by your functions. Traditional server-based architectures require you to pay for instances or virtual machines, even when they are idle. In contrast, serverless functions are billed based on the number of executions and the duration of each execution (measured in milliseconds).

This cost model is particularly advantageous for applications with variable workloads or those that experience traffic spikes. You no longer need to over-provision resources for the worst-case scenario, as you only pay for the actual usage. For startups and small businesses, this can result in significant cost savings, especially when compared to traditional hosting models.

Moreover, serverless eliminates the operational costs associated with managing and maintaining servers, reducing the overhead of infrastructure management. Businesses can focus on building features and delivering value to customers without worrying about infrastructure costs.

3. Performance

Serverless architectures are designed to optimize performance. Because functions are stateless and isolated, they can be deployed and executed independently, resulting in faster response times. Cloud providers often distribute serverless functions across multiple regions, which ensures that requests are handled by the nearest server, reducing latency and improving the user experience.

Additionally, since serverless functions scale automatically based on demand, there's no risk of performance degradation during traffic spikes. The system allocates more resources as needed, ensuring that applications remain responsive even under heavy load.

While there are challenges related to "cold starts" (the time it takes to initialize a serverless function that hasn't been recently invoked), cloud providers have made significant improvements in minimizing cold start latency, particularly for popular languages like Python.

4. Simplified Infrastructure Management

Traditional applications require careful planning and management of infrastructure, including server provisioning, configuration, and maintenance. In a serverless architecture, these concerns are abstracted away. Developers no longer need to worry about server configuration, patching, or scaling. Instead, they can focus on writing code, while the cloud provider handles the underlying infrastructure.

This simplified approach reduces the complexity of managing applications and allows teams to focus on delivering features, improving user experience, and iterating on their products.

5. Rapid Development and Deployment

Serverless architectures enable rapid development and deployment. Since serverless functions are independent and stateless, they can be developed, tested, and deployed individually. This modular approach allows teams to iterate quickly, making it easier to deploy updates, bug fixes, or new features without affecting the entire application.

Serverless also integrates seamlessly with DevOps practices, such as continuous integration and continuous deployment (CI/CD). Automated deployment pipelines can be set up to test, package, and deploy serverless functions as soon as changes are made, accelerating the release process.

6. Increased Focus on Business Logic

By abstracting away the infrastructure concerns, serverless architectures allow developers to focus on writing business logic rather than managing servers or scaling concerns. This shift in focus results in faster development cycles and more efficient use of developer resources.

For instance, instead of spending time configuring and managing a database server, a developer can leverage a serverless database service like DynamoDB or Firebase. Similarly, instead of worrying about scaling an API backend, a developer can use API Gateway and AWS Lambda to automatically handle traffic spikes and scale resources accordingly.

What to Expect from This Book

This book is designed to guide beginners through the fundamentals of serverless computing, with a particular focus on using Python in serverless architectures. It covers everything from basic concepts to advanced techniques, offering practical examples and real-world use cases to solidify your understanding.

In this book, you can expect to learn:

- How to set up your development environment for Python serverless development.
- The basics of serverless architecture and how to deploy your first

serverless function using Python.

- How to integrate with cloud services like AWS Lambda, API Gateway, DynamoDB, and more.
- Best practices for designing scalable, secure, and cost-efficient serverless applications.
- Advanced topics, such as event-driven architectures, performance optimization, and monitoring.

Each chapter provides hands-on examples, so you can follow along and build your own serverless applications step-by-step. By the end of this book, you'll have the knowledge and skills to confidently develop, deploy, and manage serverless applications using Python.

How to Get the Most Out of the Examples and Code

To maximize your learning from this book, it's important to follow along with the examples and try building your own serverless functions. Here are a few tips to get the most out of the code and examples:

1. **Set Up Your Environment Early**: Before diving into the code, ensure your development environment is properly configured. This includes installing Python, setting up virtual environments, and installing the necessary libraries.
2. **Experiment with the Code**: Don't just copy and paste the examples. Try to modify the code, experiment with different parameters, and test the behavior. This will help you gain a deeper understanding of how serverless functions work and how to troubleshoot issues.
3. **Follow Best Practices**: Pay attention to the best practices outlined in each chapter. This includes writing clean, maintainable code, managing dependencies, and securing your applications. Following these practices will help you build reliable and scalable serverless applications.
4. **Ask Questions**: If you encounter issues or have questions, don't hesitate to seek help. There are many online communities and forums

dedicated to serverless computing and Python development. Engaging with the community can help you overcome obstacles and accelerate your learning.

5. **Build Projects Along the Way**: As you progress through the book, challenge yourself to build real-world projects using the concepts you've learned. Whether it's an API, a chatbot, or a serverless automation script, applying your knowledge in practical projects will reinforce your understanding and help you gain confidence.

Chapter 1 Understanding the Serverless Computing Paradigm

Serverless computing is revolutionizing the way developers and businesses build, deploy, and manage applications. It's an architecture that abstracts away the complexities of server management, allowing developers to focus on writing and deploying code without worrying about the underlying infrastructure. In serverless computing, the cloud provider takes care of the infrastructure, scaling, and resource management, while you focus on delivering business logic.

At its core, serverless computing is about enabling developers to write and deploy small, modular functions that run in response to specific events. These functions execute independently, scale automatically, and you only pay for the compute time your functions actually use. Unlike traditional server-based architectures where you manage the infrastructure, serverless computing shifts the responsibility of scaling and managing resources to the cloud provider.

To understand the serverless paradigm, it's helpful to break it down into its fundamental components:

1. **Functions as a Service (FaaS)**: The cornerstone of serverless computing, FaaS allows you to deploy individual functions that execute in response to events. These functions are stateless, meaning they

don't retain information between invocations, and they run only when triggered by specific events, such as HTTP requests, database updates, or file uploads. We'll dive deeper into FaaS in a later section.

2. **Backend as a Service (BaaS)**: In addition to FaaS, serverless also incorporates Backend as a Service. BaaS refers to fully managed services like databases, storage, and authentication that eliminate the need to manage servers for backend operations. Examples of BaaS include Firebase, AWS Cognito, and AWS S3.

Serverless computing offers several key benefits that are driving its adoption, including automatic scaling, cost efficiency, and simplified infrastructure management. Before we explore these benefits in detail, it's essential to understand how serverless computing differs from traditional architectures.

Why Serverless?

The rise of serverless computing is part of a broader shift toward cloud-native development, where applications are built to take full advantage of cloud computing models. Cloud computing, in its simplest form, allows developers to rent computing resources (such as servers, storage, and networking) from cloud providers like Amazon Web Services (AWS), Google Cloud, and Microsoft Azure. These providers offer a range of services that developers can use to build and deploy applications without managing physical hardware.

In traditional cloud architectures, developers often use **Infrastructure as a Service (IaaS)** or **Platform as a Service (PaaS)** offerings. With IaaS, developers can rent virtual machines and configure them as needed. PaaS abstracts even more of the infrastructure, providing ready-to-use environments for running applications. However, both models still require developers to think about scaling, server configurations, and maintenance to some extent.

Serverless computing takes this abstraction to the next level. With serverless, developers don't think about servers at all. The infrastructure is entirely abstracted, and the cloud provider manages all the complexities of scaling, patching, and load balancing. Developers write code in the form of

11

functions, upload them to the cloud, and the provider handles the rest.

The most popular use case for serverless is deploying microservices and API backends, but the paradigm extends beyond that. Serverless can be used for real-time data processing, automation, machine learning, and much more.

In a nutshell, serverless allows developers to focus on writing code rather than managing infrastructure, offering a more streamlined and efficient development experience.

Key Concepts: Functions as a Service (FaaS) and Backend as a Service (BaaS)

Functions as a Service (FaaS)

The core of serverless computing is **Functions as a Service (FaaS)**. FaaS enables developers to deploy individual functions that automatically scale based on demand and run only when triggered. This shift in how code is deployed and executed eliminates the need to provision and maintain servers, allowing developers to focus purely on business logic.

A FaaS function is stateless and ephemeral—it runs in response to a specific event and is terminated once it completes execution. Common events that trigger FaaS functions include:

- **HTTP requests**: When a user makes an API request, the serverless function is invoked to handle the request and return a response.
- **Database changes**: When data is added, updated, or deleted in a database, the function can trigger to perform a related task, such as updating an analytics dashboard.
- **File uploads**: When a user uploads a file (e.g., to AWS S3 or Google Cloud Storage), the function can process the file, such as resizing an image or analyzing the contents.
- **Scheduled events**: Functions can be set to run on a schedule, much like a traditional cron job.

The serverless provider is responsible for invoking the function in response to an event, executing the function, scaling the function automatically to handle multiple invocations, and then deallocating resources once the function is done running.

Characteristics of FaaS:

1. **Event-Driven**: Functions are triggered by events such as API requests, database changes, file uploads, or scheduled tasks.
2. **Stateless**: Functions don't retain state between invocations. If state is required, it must be stored in a separate service like a database or cache.
3. **Ephemeral**: Functions only run when invoked, and they terminate as soon as the task is complete.
4. **Automatic Scaling**: The cloud provider handles scaling, ensuring that your function can handle spikes in traffic without intervention.
5. **Cost-Efficient**: With FaaS, you only pay for the execution time of your functions. When your function is idle, you aren't billed.

Popular FaaS Providers:

- **AWS Lambda**: The most popular FaaS platform, allowing developers to run code in response to AWS services like S3, DynamoDB, or API Gateway.
- **Google Cloud Functions**: Google's FaaS offering, integrated with services like Cloud Pub/Sub, Cloud Storage, and Firebase.
- **Microsoft Azure Functions**: Azure's FaaS platform that integrates with Azure services like Cosmos DB, Event Grid, and Logic Apps.

Backend as a Service (BaaS)

In addition to FaaS, serverless computing often relies on **Backend as a Service (BaaS)**. BaaS refers to fully managed backend services that developers can leverage without managing the underlying servers. These services typically include databases, storage, authentication, and messaging services.

BaaS provides ready-to-use backend functionality, such as:

- **Database as a Service**: Managed databases like AWS DynamoDB, Google Firebase, and Azure Cosmos DB provide scalable, serverless databases.
- **Authentication as a Service**: Services like AWS Cognito and Firebase Authentication allow developers to implement user authentication and authorization without building their own identity management systems.
- **File Storage as a Service**: Services like AWS S3 and Google Cloud Storage provide scalable file storage for applications without the need to manage storage servers.
- **Messaging as a Service**: Services like AWS SNS, Google Cloud Pub/Sub, and Azure Service Bus allow applications to communicate asynchronously via messaging queues.

BaaS services complement FaaS functions by providing the necessary backend infrastructure for your application. For example, you could use AWS Lambda (FaaS) to process an image when it's uploaded to S3 (BaaS). Or you could use Firebase Cloud Functions (FaaS) to validate user data before writing it to Firebase Realtime Database (BaaS).

Advantages of BaaS:

- **No Server Management**: BaaS providers manage all aspects of the backend infrastructure, including scaling, patching, and maintenance.
- **Seamless Integration**: BaaS services are designed to integrate with FaaS functions and other cloud services, enabling developers to build scalable, modular applications quickly.
- **Cost-Effective**: Like FaaS, BaaS services follow a pay-as-you-go model, ensuring that you only pay for the resources you use.

Serverless vs. Traditional Architectures

Serverless computing is often compared to traditional architectures, such as **monolithic** and **microservice** architectures. While traditional architectures have been effective for many years, serverless introduces a new level of abstraction and flexibility that offers distinct advantages for certain types of applications.

Traditional Monolithic Architecture

In a traditional monolithic architecture, an application is built as a single, self-contained unit. All of the application's components—such as the user interface, business logic, and data access—are tightly coupled and deployed as a single unit.

- **Advantages of Monolithic Architecture**:
- Simple to develop and deploy, particularly for small applications.
- Easier to test and manage, as everything is in one codebase.
- Suitable for applications with low complexity and few scaling requirements.
- **Disadvantages of Monolithic Architecture**:
- Hard to scale. Since all components are tightly coupled, scaling individual components independently is difficult.
- Difficult to maintain and update, particularly as the application grows in size and complexity.
- A failure in one part of the application can bring down the entire system.

Microservices Architecture

Microservices architecture evolved as a solution to the limitations of monolithic architecture. In a microservices architecture, an application is divided into independent services, each responsible for a specific business capability. Each microservice is developed, deployed, and scaled independently.

- **Advantages of Microservices Architecture**:
- Scalability: Microservices can scale independently, allowing you to

allocate resources where needed.

- Flexibility: Different teams can work on different microservices, using different programming languages or frameworks if necessary.
- Fault isolation: If one microservice fails, it doesn't necessarily affect the others.
- **Disadvantages of Microservices Architecture**:
- Increased complexity: Managing multiple services introduces complexity in terms of communication, data consistency, and deployment.
- Requires robust infrastructure: You need to implement communication protocols (e.g., REST, gRPC) and service discovery mechanisms.
- Monitoring and debugging: Debugging and monitoring distributed systems are more challenging than in a monolithic system.

Serverless Architecture

Serverless architecture takes the microservices concept one step further by abstracting away the infrastructure management entirely. In serverless architecture, developers write individual functions that execute in response to events and are managed entirely by the cloud provider.

- **Advantages of Serverless Architecture**:
- **No server management**: You don't need to worry about provisioning, configuring, or maintaining servers. The cloud provider handles everything.
- **Automatic scaling**: Serverless functions automatically scale based on demand, ensuring that your application can handle spikes in traffic.
- **Cost-efficient**: You only pay for the actual compute time your functions use. When your application is idle, you're not charged for idle resources.
- **Modular development**: Functions are independent and stateless, making it easier to develop and maintain specific pieces of logic.
- **Disadvantages of Serverless Architecture**:
- **Cold starts**: Serverless functions can experience cold starts when they haven't been invoked recently. This can introduce latency for the first invocation.

- **Stateless nature**: Since serverless functions are stateless, managing state across multiple invocations requires external storage solutions (e.g., databases, caches).
- **Vendor lock-in**: Serverless platforms are tightly integrated with specific cloud providers, making it difficult to migrate to another platform.

In general, serverless architecture is ideal for applications that require high scalability, have unpredictable workloads, or need to minimize operational overhead. It's especially well-suited for event-driven applications, APIs, and real-time data processing. However, for applications with constant, long-running workloads or specific performance requirements, traditional or microservice architectures may still be more appropriate.

Common Serverless Platforms: AWS Lambda, Google Cloud Functions, Azure Functions

Several cloud providers offer serverless platforms, each with its own set of features and services. While AWS Lambda is the most widely known, Google Cloud Functions and Microsoft Azure Functions are also popular choices for developers looking to build serverless applications. Let's explore the three most popular serverless platforms.

1. AWS Lambda

AWS Lambda is the most popular and widely used serverless platform. Introduced by Amazon Web Services in 2014, Lambda allows developers to run code in response to various events, such as HTTP requests, file uploads to S3, or updates to a database.

- **Key Features**:
- Supports multiple programming languages, including Python, Node.js, Java, C#, and Ruby.
- Integrated with AWS services like S3, DynamoDB, API Gateway, SNS, and SQS.
- Automatic scaling: Lambda functions automatically scale to handle

increasing loads.

- Pay-per-use pricing: You only pay for the compute time your functions use (billed in milliseconds).
- Supports asynchronous and synchronous invocation.
- **Use Cases**:
- Building APIs with API Gateway and Lambda.
- Processing files uploaded to S3 (e.g., image processing, data analysis).
- Real-time data processing and analytics.
- Automated task execution, such as running scheduled jobs (using AWS CloudWatch Events).
- **Advantages**:
- Tight integration with the AWS ecosystem.
- Highly scalable and reliable platform.
- Extensive documentation and community support.

2. Google Cloud Functions

Google Cloud Functions is Google's FaaS offering, which allows developers to run event-driven functions in response to various Google Cloud services. Cloud Functions are ideal for building lightweight, event-driven applications that need to scale automatically.

- **Key Features**:
- Supports multiple languages, including Python, Node.js, Go, and Java.
- Integrated with Google Cloud services like Cloud Pub/Sub, Firebase, and Cloud Storage.
- Automatic scaling based on demand.
- Pay-per-use pricing: You are only charged for the actual execution time.
- **Use Cases**:
- Processing events from Cloud Pub/Sub (Google's messaging service).
- Handling file uploads to Google Cloud Storage.
- Real-time updates to Firebase applications.
- Running lightweight APIs or microservices.
- **Advantages**:

- Seamless integration with Google Cloud's services, including Firebase and machine learning tools.
- Fast execution and low latency.
- Ideal for real-time applications and APIs.

3. Microsoft Azure Functions

Azure Functions is Microsoft's FaaS offering, allowing developers to run small pieces of code in response to events from Azure services. Azure Functions can be triggered by HTTP requests, database changes, file uploads, and other events within the Azure ecosystem.

- **Key Features**:
- Supports a wide range of languages, including Python, C#, JavaScript, and Java.
- Integrated with Azure services like Cosmos DB, Event Grid, and Logic Apps.
- Automatic scaling based on demand.
- Pay-per-use pricing, billed based on execution time.
- **Use Cases**:
- Building serverless APIs with HTTP triggers.
- Processing events from Azure Event Grid and Azure Storage.
- Running scheduled tasks and automated workflows.
- Real-time data processing and analytics.
- **Advantages**:
- Deep integration with Microsoft Azure's cloud services.
- Support for a wide range of programming languages.
- Flexible pricing and scaling options.

Conclusion

In this chapter, we explored the foundational concepts of serverless computing, including Functions as a Service (FaaS) and Backend as a Service (BaaS). We also compared serverless architecture with traditional and microservices architectures, highlighting the advantages and trade-offs of each. Finally, we reviewed the most popular serverless platforms—AWS Lambda, Google Cloud Functions, and Microsoft Azure Functions.

By understanding the basics of serverless computing, you are now ready to dive into the practical aspects of building serverless applications with Python. In the next chapter, we will explore why Python is the perfect language for serverless development and begin setting up your development environment.

Chapter 2: Python and Serverless: A Perfect Match

S erverless computing is one of the most transformative trends in modern software development, and Python is ideally suited for this architecture. As developers transition to serverless architectures to simplify infrastructure management, Python emerges as a top choice due to its versatility, ease of use, and integration with major cloud platforms. In this chapter, we'll explore why Python is perfect for serverless computing, set up the necessary tools and environment for developing serverless applications with Python, and walk through writing your first Python function for serverless deployment.

Why Python is Ideal for Serverless Computing

Serverless computing is all about abstracting infrastructure management and focusing solely on writing code that can be executed on demand. Python's inherent strengths, including its readability, speed of development, and broad ecosystem of libraries, make it an ideal language for building serverless applications. Here are some key reasons why Python is particularly well-suited for serverless computing.

1. Easy-to-Learn and Readable Syntax

Python is often praised for its simple and clean syntax, which makes it accessible to beginners while also being powerful enough for seasoned developers. In the context of serverless computing, where developers need to write functions that respond to events in the cloud, Python's straightforward syntax allows for rapid development and deployment.

The readability of Python reduces the cognitive load on developers, enabling them to focus on solving problems rather than getting bogged down by complex language constructs. This is especially beneficial in serverless development, where the focus is on writing small, modular functions that are easy to understand and maintain.

2. Fast Prototyping and Development

One of Python's most compelling features is its ability to allow fast prototyping. Because serverless functions are often short, self-contained pieces of logic, Python's flexibility and speed in development become an asset. This allows developers to quickly experiment with new ideas and deploy changes with minimal overhead.

Python's dynamic nature, along with its high-level abstractions, enables developers to write fewer lines of code compared to languages like Java or C#. This reduces the development time, making it possible to go from an idea to a working serverless function in a short span of time.

3. Extensive Library Support

Python's vast ecosystem of libraries is another key reason why it's a popular choice for serverless computing. Python has libraries for nearly every conceivable task, from handling HTTP requests to interacting with cloud services, processing data, and even running machine learning models.

In serverless architectures, where efficiency is paramount, being able to leverage pre-existing libraries can significantly accelerate development. For instance, if you're building a serverless API on AWS Lambda, Python's **Boto3** library makes it easy to interact with AWS services like S3, DynamoDB, and API Gateway.

Additionally, popular libraries such as **Requests** for HTTP interactions, **NumPy** for numerical computing, and **Pandas** for data manipulation provide robust functionality, enabling developers to write high-quality, efficient code for serverless applications.

4. Python's Cross-Platform Compatibility

Python is a cross-platform language, meaning code written in Python can run on multiple operating systems, including Windows, macOS, and Linux. In serverless computing, where functions may need to run in diverse cloud environments, Python's portability ensures that your code can be deployed across different platforms without modification.

Cloud platforms like AWS Lambda, Google Cloud Functions, and Microsoft Azure Functions all provide native support for Python, making it easy to write and deploy Python functions on any major cloud provider. This cross-platform compatibility further strengthens Python's position as an ideal language for serverless development.

5. Strong Support for Asynchronous Programming

Serverless architectures are often event-driven and require handling a large number of concurrent requests. Python's support for asynchronous programming with **asyncio** makes it particularly well-suited for building scalable, event-driven applications.

With **asyncio**, Python enables non-blocking I/O operations, allowing serverless functions to efficiently handle high volumes of requests without getting bogged down by slow operations like network requests or database interactions. This asynchronous capability is crucial in serverless environments, where minimizing execution time and maximizing throughput are essential to cost and performance optimization.

6. Integration with Major Cloud Platforms

Python's compatibility with major cloud providers is another factor that makes it an excellent choice for serverless development. AWS Lambda, Google Cloud Functions, and Azure Functions all support Python as a first-class citizen, providing SDKs and tools specifically designed for developing Python-based serverless applications.

For instance, **Boto3**, the AWS SDK for Python, makes it simple to interact with AWS services programmatically. Similarly, Google Cloud offers the **google-cloud** library for Python developers, enabling seamless interaction with Google Cloud services such as Cloud Pub/Sub, Cloud Storage, and Firebase. This deep integration with cloud platforms makes Python a natural fit for serverless applications.

Installing Python and Setting Up Your Development Environment

Before we dive into writing and deploying Python serverless functions, it's essential to set up your local development environment. In this section, we'll walk through the steps of installing Python, configuring your development environment, and setting up the necessary tools for serverless development.

Step 1: Installing Python

Python is available for all major operating systems, including Windows, macOS, and Linux. If you don't already have Python installed on your system, follow these steps to install it:

1. **Download Python**:

- Visit the official Python website at https://www.python.org/download s/.
- Download the latest stable version of Python (preferably Python 3.x) for your operating system.

1. **Install Python**:

- Follow the instructions specific to your operating system:
- **Windows**: Run the installer and make sure to check the box labeled "Add Python to PATH" during installation. This will allow you to run Python from the command line.
- **macOS**: macOS comes with a pre-installed version of Python, but it's often outdated. You can install the latest version using Homebrew:

```bash
Copy code
brew install python
```

- **Linux**: Most Linux distributions come with Python pre-installed. However, you can update Python using your package manager:

```bash
Copy code
sudo apt-get install python3
```

1. **Verify Installation**:

- Once Python is installed, open a terminal or command prompt and verify the installation by running the following command:

```bash
Copy code
python --version
```

- This command should return the version number of Python installed on your system.

Step 2: Installing pip (Python Package Installer)

Python comes with a package manager called **pip**, which allows you to install additional libraries and dependencies for your projects. In most cases, pip is installed automatically with Python. You can verify if pip is installed by running the following command:

```bash
Copy code
pip --version
```

If pip is not installed, you can install it manually by following the instructions on the official Python website or using the following command:

```bash
Copy code
python -m ensurepip --upgrade
```

Once pip is installed, you can use it to install Python packages and libraries that are essential for serverless development.

Introduction to Virtual Environments and Dependency Management (pip, virtualenv)

In Python development, managing dependencies is crucial, especially when working on multiple projects. Different projects may require different versions of libraries, and it's important to keep them isolated to avoid conflicts. This is where virtual environments come in.

What is a Virtual Environment?

A **virtual environment** is an isolated environment that contains its own Python interpreter and dependencies. It allows you to create a self-contained directory for a project, where you can install specific versions of libraries without affecting the global Python environment.

Using virtual environments ensures that the dependencies required by one project don't interfere with those of another. This is especially useful when working with serverless applications, where you may need to install specific versions of libraries to ensure compatibility with cloud platforms like AWS Lambda or Google Cloud Functions.

Setting Up a Virtual Environment

To create and manage virtual environments, Python provides a built-in module called venv. Additionally, you can use a third-party tool called **virtualenv**, which offers more features and flexibility.

1. **Creating a Virtual Environment with venv**:

- To create a virtual environment using the venv module, open a terminal or command prompt and navigate to your project directory. Then run the following command:

```bash
Copy code
python -m venv myenv
```

- This command creates a new virtual environment named myenv in your project directory.

1. **Activating the Virtual Environment**:

- After creating the virtual environment, you need to activate it. The activation process is different for each operating system:
- **Windows**:

```bash
Copy code
myenv\Scripts\activate
```

- **macOS/Linux**:

```bash
Copy code
source myenv/bin/activate
```

- Once the virtual environment is activated, you'll notice that the terminal prompt changes to indicate that you're working within the virtual environment.

1. **Installing Dependencies**:

- After activating the virtual environment, you can use pip to install dependencies. For example, to install the requests library, run the following command:

```bash
Copy code
pip install requests
```

1. **Deactivating the Virtual Environment**:

- When you're done working on your project, you can deactivate the virtual environment by running the following command:

```bash
Copy code
deactivate
```

By using virtual environments, you can keep your projects organized and ensure that the dependencies for each project are isolated and manageable.

Writing Your First Python Function for Serverless

Now that you've set up your development environment

4o

ChatGPT said:

ChatGPT

and understood the importance of virtual environments, it's time to write your first Python function for serverless deployment. In this section, we'll create a simple serverless function that responds to HTTP requests using AWS Lambda and the AWS API Gateway.

Step 1: Setting Up AWS CLI and Serverless Framework

To deploy serverless applications to AWS, it's helpful to use the **AWS Command Line Interface (CLI)** and the **Serverless Framework**. The AWS CLI allows you to interact with AWS services from your terminal, while the Serverless Framework simplifies the process of deploying serverless applications.

1. **Install AWS CLI**:

* You can install the AWS CLI using pip:

```bash
Copy code
pip install awscli
```

1. **Configure AWS CLI**:

* After installation, you need to configure the AWS CLI with your AWS credentials. Run the following command:

```bash
Copy code
aws configure
```

- You'll be prompted to enter your AWS Access Key ID, Secret Access Key, region, and output format. You can find your access keys in the AWS Management Console under IAM (Identity and Access Management).

1. **Install Serverless Framework**:

- The Serverless Framework can be installed globally using npm (Node Package Manager). First, ensure that you have Node.js installed, and then run the following command:

```bash
Copy code
npm install -g serverless
```

1. **Create a New Serverless Project**:

- Navigate to the directory where you want to create your project and run:

```bash
Copy code
serverless create --template aws-python --path my-serverless-app
```

- This command creates a new serverless application using the AWS Python template in a directory named my-serverless-app.

Step 2: Understanding the Project Structure

Navigate to your newly created project directory (my-serverless-app). You'll find a few important files:

- **serverless.yml**: This is the configuration file where you define your serverless service, including functions, events, and resources.
- **handler.py**: This file contains your Python functions that will be deployed to AWS Lambda.
- **requirements.txt**: This file lists the Python dependencies for your serverless application.

Step 3: Writing Your First Python Function

Open the handler.py file in your preferred code editor. You'll see a basic structure for a Lambda function. Let's modify it to create a simple HTTP endpoint that responds with a greeting.

Replace the existing code in handler.py with the following:

```python
Copy code
def hello(event, context):
    name = event.get("queryStringParameters",
{}).get("name", "World")
    return {
        "statusCode": 200,
        "body": f"Hello, {name}!"
    }
```

This function checks for a query parameter named name. If it exists, it responds with a personalized greeting; otherwise, it defaults to "World."

Step 4: Configuring the Function in serverless.yml

Now, open the serverless.yml file to configure your function and set up the API Gateway trigger. The file should look like this:

```yaml
yaml
Copy code
service: my-serverless-app

provider:
  name: aws
  runtime: python3.8

functions:
  hello:
    handler: handler.hello
    events:
      - http:
          path: hello
          method: get
```

In this configuration:

- We define the service name (my-serverless-app).
- We specify AWS as the provider and set the runtime to Python 3.8.
- We declare a function named hello, which points to the hello function in handler.py.
- We set up an HTTP event that triggers the function when a GET request is made to the /hello path.

Step 5: Deploying Your Serverless Function

With the function written and the configuration set up, you're ready to deploy your serverless application to AWS. From the terminal, navigate to your project directory and run:

```bash
bash
Copy code
serverless deploy
```

The Serverless Framework will package your application, create the necessary resources on AWS (including the Lambda function and API Gateway), and deploy everything to your AWS account. After the deployment completes, you'll see an endpoint URL in the output.

Step 6: Testing Your Function

To test your serverless function, open a web browser or a tool like Postman and navigate to the endpoint URL provided by the Serverless Framework. You can append a query parameter to the URL to customize the greeting:

```php
Copy code
https://<api-id>.
execute-api.<region>.
amazonaws.com/dev/hello?name=John
```

Replace <api-id> and <region> with the values specific to your deployment. When you access this URL, you should see the response:

```
Copy code
Hello, John!
```

If you visit the URL without the name parameter:

```php
Copy code
https://<api-id>.execute
-api.<region>.
amazonaws.com/dev/hello
```

You should receive:

```
Copy code
Hello, World!
```

Step 7: Cleaning Up

After testing, it's good practice to clean up your resources to avoid unnecessary charges on your AWS account. You can remove the deployed service by running:

```bash
Copy code
serverless remove
```

This command deletes all resources created during the deployment process.

Conclusion

In this chapter, we explored why Python is an ideal language for serverless computing, emphasizing its ease of use, extensive library support, and strong integration with cloud platforms. We also covered the steps to install Python, set up a development environment, and manage dependencies using virtual environments.

Finally, we wrote our first serverless function in Python, deployed it to AWS Lambda, and tested it using the API Gateway. With this foundation in place, you are well-prepared to explore more advanced serverless concepts and develop robust serverless applications using Python. In the next chapter, we will delve deeper into the specific features of AWS Lambda and how to harness its full potential in your serverless projects.

Chapter 3: Exploring the Serverless Framework

Serverless computing has transformed the way developers build and deploy applications, enabling them to focus on writing code while abstracting away the underlying infrastructure. The Serverless Framework (often abbreviated as SLS) is a powerful tool that simplifies the development and deployment of serverless applications across multiple cloud providers, such as AWS, Google Cloud, and Azure. In this chapter, we will explore the Serverless Framework in detail, including its features, installation process, configuration files, and the steps to deploy your first serverless application.

Introduction to the Serverless Framework (SLS)

The Serverless Framework is an open-source framework that enables developers to build and manage serverless applications easily. It was created to simplify the complexities involved in developing and deploying serverless architectures, making it accessible for both beginners and experienced developers. The framework provides a consistent way to define, configure, and deploy serverless functions and services across different cloud providers.

Key Features of the Serverless Framework

1. **Multi-Cloud Support**: The Serverless Framework supports multiple cloud providers, including AWS Lambda, Google Cloud Functions, Azure Functions, and more. This allows developers to write applications that can be easily deployed across different environments, providing flexibility and avoiding vendor lock-in.

2. **Infrastructure as Code**: The framework uses configuration files (typically named serverless.yml) to define the infrastructure for your serverless application. This Infrastructure as Code (IaC) approach allows you to version control your infrastructure, making it easier to manage and collaborate with others.

3. **Ecosystem of Plugins**: The Serverless Framework has a rich ecosystem of plugins that extend its functionality. These plugins can add features like monitoring, debugging, and custom deployment strategies, allowing developers to tailor the framework to their specific needs.

4. **Easy Deployment**: With a simple command-line interface, the Serverless Framework simplifies the deployment process. Developers can deploy their entire application stack with a single command, automating the creation of cloud resources and configurations.

5. **Event-Driven Architecture**: The framework is designed to work seamlessly with event-driven architectures, enabling developers to define events that trigger their serverless functions. This is particularly useful for building applications that respond to real-time events, such as API requests, file uploads, or database changes.

6. **Support for Environment Variables**: The Serverless Framework allows you to define environment variables for your functions, making it easy to manage configurations and secrets. This feature enhances the security and flexibility of your serverless applications.

7. **Built-In Monitoring and Debugging**: Many plugins and tools are available within the Serverless ecosystem that can provide monitoring, logging, and debugging capabilities for your serverless applications. This helps developers troubleshoot issues quickly and maintain the

reliability of their applications.

By leveraging these features, the Serverless Framework enables developers to focus on writing business logic rather than managing infrastructure, leading to faster development cycles and improved productivity.

Installing and Setting Up the Serverless Framework

Before you can start using the Serverless Framework, you need to install it on your local machine. In this section, we will guide you through the installation process and help you set up the Serverless Framework for your development environment.

Step 1: Prerequisites

Before installing the Serverless Framework, make sure you have the following prerequisites:

1. **Node.js**: The Serverless Framework is built on Node.js, so you need to have Node.js installed on your machine. You can download the latest version of Node.js from https://nodejs.org/.
2. **npm**: npm (Node Package Manager) comes bundled with Node.js and is used to install the Serverless Framework.
3. **AWS CLI**: If you plan to deploy serverless applications on AWS, make sure you have the AWS Command Line Interface (CLI) installed and configured with your AWS credentials. You can refer to the previous chapter for instructions on installing and configuring the AWS CLI.

Step 2: Installing the Serverless Framework

Once you have the prerequisites in place, you can install the Serverless Framework using npm. Open your terminal or command prompt and run the following command:

```
bash
Copy code
npm install -g serverless
```

This command installs the Serverless Framework globally on your machine, allowing you to access it from any directory. Once the installation is complete, you can verify that the Serverless Framework is installed by running:

```
bash
Copy code
serverless --version
```

You should see the version number of the Serverless Framework printed in the terminal, indicating that the installation was successful.

Step 3: Setting Up Your First Serverless Project

With the Serverless Framework installed, you can create your first serverless project. The framework provides a command to scaffold new projects using templates. In this example, we will create a simple serverless application using the AWS provider.

1. **Create a New Serverless Service**: Navigate to the directory where you want to create your project, and run the following command:

```
bash
Copy code
serverless create --template
 aws-python --path my-serverless-app
```

1. This command creates a new serverless application named my-serverless-app using the AWS Python template.
2. **Navigate to Your Project Directory**: After creating the project, navigate into the project directory:

```bash
Copy code
cd my-serverless-app
```

Step 4: Exploring the Project Structure

In the my-serverless-app directory, you will find several important files:

- **serverless.yml**: This is the main configuration file where you define your serverless service, including functions, events, and resources.
- **handler.py**: This file contains your Python functions that will be deployed to AWS Lambda.
- **requirements.txt**: This file lists the Python dependencies for your serverless application.
- **.gitignore**: This file specifies files and directories to ignore when using Git for version control.

Let's take a closer look at the key components of the serverless.yml configuration file.

Configuration Files (serverless.yml)

The serverless.yml file is a crucial component of the Serverless Framework. It serves as the blueprint for your serverless application, allowing you to define the functions, events, and resources that comprise your application. Understanding how to configure this file is essential for effective serverless development.

Basic Structure of serverless.yml

Here's a basic structure of a serverless.yml file:

```yaml
Copy code
service: my-serverless-app

provider:
  name: aws
  runtime: python3.8

functions:
  hello:
    handler: handler.hello
    events:
      - http:
          path: hello
          method: get
```

Key Sections of serverless.yml

1. **Service Name**: The service property defines the name of your server-less service. This name is used to create a CloudFormation stack and uniquely identify your application within your cloud provider.
2. **Provider**: The provider section specifies the cloud provider you are using (e.g., AWS, Google Cloud, Azure) and the runtime environment for your functions. In the example above, we are using AWS as the provider and Python 3.8 as the runtime.
3. **Functions**: The functions section defines the individual serverless functions that make up your application. Each function must have a unique name (in this case, hello) and specify the handler (the function to invoke) and the events that trigger it.
4. **Events**: Events determine how the function is invoked. In the example,

the function is triggered by an HTTP GET request to the /hello endpoint. You can define multiple events for a single function.

5. **Resources** (Optional): You can define additional cloud resources that your serverless application requires, such as databases, queues, or S3 buckets, using the resources section. This section allows you to leverage AWS CloudFormation templates for resource management.

Defining Environment Variables

In the serverless.yml file, you can define environment variables that your functions can access. Environment variables are useful for storing configuration settings, secrets, or API keys. Here's how to define environment variables in the configuration file:

```yaml
Copy code
provider:
  name: aws
  runtime: python3.8
  environment:
    MY_API_KEY: your_api_key_here
```

In your Python code, you can access the environment variables using the os module:

```python
Copy code
import os

def hello(event, context):
    api_key = os.environ.get("MY_API_KEY")
    return {
        "statusCode": 200,
        "body": f"My API key is {api_key}"
    }
```

Configuring Resources

If your application requires additional resources, you can define them in the resources section. For example, if you need to create an S3 bucket, you can do it like this:

```yaml
Copy code
resources:
  Resources:
    MyS3Bucket:
      Type: AWS::S3::Bucket
      Properties:
        BucketName: my-unique-bucket-name
```

By defining resources in your serverless.yml file, you ensure that they are created automatically when you deploy your application, keeping everything managed in one place.

Deploying Your First Serverless Application

Now that we have our serverless application configured, it's time to deploy it to AWS using the Serverless Framework. In this section, we'll go through the steps to deploy your application and test the endpoint.

Step 1: Deploying the Application

To deploy your serverless application, navigate to your project directory (if you haven't already) and run the following command:

```bash
Copy code
serverless deploy
```

During the deployment process, the Serverless Framework will:

- Package your application and its dependencies.
- Create the necessary resources in AWS (Lambda functions, API Gateway, etc.).
- Generate a CloudFormation stack that manages your resources.

Once the deployment is complete, you'll see an output similar to the following:

```yaml
Copy code
Service Information
service: my-serverless-app
stage: dev
region: us-east-1
stack: my-serverless-app-dev
resources: 12
api keys:
  None
endpoints:
  GET -
  https://<api-id>.execute-api.us-east-1.amazonaws.com/dev/hello
functions:
  hello: my-serverless-app-dev-hello
```

Step 2: Testing the Endpoint

With the deployment complete, you can now test the endpoint created by the Serverless Framework. Open a web browser or use a tool like Postman and navigate to the endpoint URL provided in the deployment output:

```arduino
Copy code
https://<api-id>.
execute-api.us-east-1.
amazonaws.com/dev/hello
```

You can also append a query parameter to the URL to customize the greeting:

```
arduino
Copy code
https://<api-id>.
execute-api.us-east-1.
amazonaws.com/dev/hello?name=Alice
```

You should see a response similar to the following:

```
Copy code
Hello, Alice!
```

If you access the endpoint without the name parameter, you should receive the default greeting:

```
Copy code
Hello, World!
```

Step 3: Monitoring and Logs

One of the powerful features of the Serverless Framework is its ability to monitor and manage your serverless functions. You can view logs and metrics to ensure that your functions are running smoothly.

To view logs for your deployed function, you can use the following command:

```
bash
Copy code
serverless logs -f hello
```

This command retrieves the logs for the hello function, allowing you to debug any issues or monitor the function's performance.

Step 4: Updating Your Function

As you develop your application, you may need to make changes to your function. To update your function, simply modify the code in handler.py and then redeploy your application using the following command:

```bash
Copy code
serverless deploy
```

The Serverless Framework will handle the updates and redeploy only the modified functions, ensuring that your application remains up-to-date without downtime.

Step 5: Cleaning Up Resources

Once you're done experimenting with your serverless application, it's important to clean up the resources you created to avoid incurring costs. You can remove the deployed service and all associated resources by running:

```bash
Copy code
serverless remove
```

This command deletes the CloudFormation stack and all resources created during the deployment process.

Conclusion

In this chapter, we explored the Serverless Framework and its significance in serverless development. We discussed its key features, including multi-cloud support, Infrastructure as Code, and the ability to simplify deployment processes. We also walked through the steps to install the Serverless

Framework, create a new project, configure the serverless.yml file, and deploy your first serverless application.

By leveraging the Serverless Framework, you can streamline your serverless development workflow and take full advantage of serverless computing's benefits. In the next chapter, we will dive deeper into AWS Lambda, exploring its features, performance optimization techniques, and best practices for building serverless applications with Python.

Chapter 4: Understanding AWS Lambda

As one of the cornerstone services of Amazon Web Services (AWS), AWS Lambda revolutionizes the way developers build and manage applications in the cloud. By allowing developers to run code in response to events without provisioning or managing servers, AWS Lambda empowers businesses to build scalable, efficient, and cost-effective applications. In this chapter, we will explore AWS Lambda in depth, covering its core concepts, how to write and deploy Python functions, and providing a hands-on example to illustrate its capabilities.

What is AWS Lambda?

AWS Lambda is a serverless compute service that allows developers to run code in response to events without the need to provision or manage servers. With Lambda, you can execute code for virtually any type of application or backend service with zero administration. This means you can focus on writing your application code without worrying about server maintenance, scaling, or infrastructure management.

Key Features of AWS Lambda

1. **Event-Driven Execution**: AWS Lambda functions are triggered by events from various AWS services and external sources. This event-driven model allows you to respond to real-time changes in your application environment, making it ideal for building reactive systems.

2. **Automatic Scaling**: Lambda automatically scales your application by running code in response to incoming requests. Each request is processed independently, and Lambda can handle thousands of requests simultaneously without requiring you to configure or manage the underlying infrastructure.

3. **Flexible Resource Allocation**: When you define a Lambda function, you can specify the amount of memory allocated to it, which directly affects the CPU performance. You can adjust these settings based on the workload requirements of your function, allowing for optimized resource usage.

4. **Cost Efficiency**: With AWS Lambda, you pay only for the compute time you consume. You are charged based on the number of requests and the duration of your function's execution, measured in milliseconds. This pay-as-you-go model allows for significant cost savings, particularly for applications with variable workloads.

5. **Integration with AWS Services**: AWS Lambda integrates seamlessly with various AWS services, including Amazon S3, DynamoDB, API Gateway, SNS, SQS, and more. This integration makes it easy to build complex applications that leverage the full power of the AWS ecosystem.

6. **Support for Multiple Languages**: AWS Lambda natively supports multiple programming languages, including Python, Node.js, Java, C#, Go, Ruby, and PowerShell. This allows developers to use their preferred languages while building serverless applications.

7. **Security and Compliance**: AWS Lambda operates within a secure environment, and you can configure access permissions using AWS Identity and Access Management (IAM). You can control which AWS resources your Lambda function can access, ensuring compliance with

security policies.

8. **Monitoring and Logging**: AWS Lambda integrates with Amazon CloudWatch to provide monitoring and logging capabilities. You can track the performance of your functions, view logs, and set up alerts to monitor application health.

Key AWS Lambda Concepts: Event-Driven Architecture

AWS Lambda operates on the principle of event-driven architecture, where actions are triggered by events from various sources. Understanding this architecture is crucial to effectively utilizing AWS Lambda and building responsive, scalable applications.

Event Sources

AWS Lambda can be triggered by a variety of event sources, including:

1. **HTTP Requests**: When integrated with Amazon API Gateway, Lambda functions can be invoked by HTTP requests. This allows you to create RESTful APIs and microservices that respond to web requests.
2. **File Uploads**: You can trigger Lambda functions in response to file uploads to Amazon S3. For example, when an image is uploaded to an S3 bucket, a Lambda function can be invoked to process the image.
3. **Database Changes**: AWS Lambda can respond to changes in DynamoDB tables. You can set up streams that trigger functions when data is added, updated, or deleted.
4. **Messaging Services**: Lambda can process messages from Amazon Simple Notification Service (SNS) or Amazon Simple Queue Service (SQS). This allows for building asynchronous workflows that respond to messages and events.
5. **Scheduled Events**: You can schedule Lambda functions to run at specific intervals using Amazon CloudWatch Events. This is useful for tasks like data processing, cleanup jobs, or periodic reports.

Invocation Types

AWS Lambda supports two primary invocation types:

1. **Synchronous Invocation**: In synchronous invocation, the caller waits for the function to complete its execution and returns the result. This is typical for HTTP requests handled by API Gateway, where the response is returned directly to the client.
2. **Asynchronous Invocation**: In asynchronous invocation, the caller does not wait for the function to complete. Instead, the request is queued for execution, and the caller receives an acknowledgment immediately. This is useful for tasks that can be processed in the background, such as sending notifications or processing data streams.

Execution Context

When a Lambda function is invoked, AWS Lambda creates an execution context that contains all the information needed to run the function. This context includes:

- **Function Configuration**: Information about the function, such as the runtime, memory allocation, and timeout settings.
- **Environment Variables**: Any environment variables defined in the serverless.yml file or in the AWS Lambda console.
- **Event Data**: The event that triggered the function, which may contain relevant information needed for processing (e.g., an HTTP request body, S3 bucket details, etc.).

The execution context is created once for each invocation, and AWS reuses the context for subsequent invocations, which can improve performance.

Writing and Deploying Python Functions to AWS Lambda

Now that we have a foundational understanding of AWS Lambda and its event-driven architecture, let's dive into the practical aspects of writing and deploying Python functions to AWS Lambda.

Step 1: Setting Up Your Project Structure

First, create a new directory for your AWS Lambda project. Navigate to your terminal and run:

```bash
Copy code
mkdir aws-lambda-python-example
cd aws-lambda-python-example
```

Within this directory, create the following files:

1. **handler.py**: This file will contain your Python function that will be deployed to AWS Lambda.
2. **requirements.txt**: This file will list any external Python dependencies your function may require.

Step 2: Writing Your Python Function

Open the handler.py file in your preferred text editor and write a simple Lambda function that responds to HTTP requests. Here's an example of a function that returns a greeting based on a name provided in the query string:

```python
Copy code
import json
```

```python
def lambda_handler(event, context):
    name = event.get("queryStringParameters", {}).get("name",
    "World")

    return {
        "statusCode": 200,
        "body": json.dumps({
            "message": f"Hello, {name}!"
        })
    }
```

In this example, the lambda_handler function extracts the name parameter from the incoming event (which will be provided by API Gateway) and returns a JSON response with a greeting message.

Step 3: Creating requirements.txt

If your function relies on external libraries, specify them in the requirements.txt file. For our simple greeting function, we don't need any external libraries, but you might want to add libraries like requests or boto3 for more complex applications.

For example:

```
Copy code
requests
```

Step 4: Creating the serverless.yml Configuration File

Now that we have our function written, we need to configure the serverless.yml file to deploy the function to AWS Lambda. Create a new file named serverless.yml in the project directory and add the following configuration:

```yaml
yaml
Copy code
service: aws-lambda-python-example

provider:
  name: aws
  runtime: python3.8

functions:
  hello:
    handler: handler.lambda_handler
    events:
      - http:
          path: hello
          method: get
```

In this configuration:

- We define the service name as aws-lambda-python-example.
- We specify AWS as the provider and set the runtime to Python 3.8.
- We declare a function named hello, which points to the lambda_handler function in handler.py.
- We set up an HTTP event that triggers the function when a GET request is made to the /hello path.

Step 5: Deploying the Function to AWS Lambda

Before deploying, make sure you have the **Serverless Framework** installed and configured, as explained in the previous chapters. Once everything is set up, you can deploy your function using the following command:

```bash
bash
Copy code
serverless deploy
```

During the deployment process, the Serverless Framework will package your application, create the necessary resources in AWS (including the Lambda function and API Gateway), and deploy everything to your AWS account. Once the deployment is complete, you'll see an endpoint URL in the output.

Step 6: Testing Your Function

To test your newly deployed Lambda function, open a web browser or a tool like Postman and navigate to the endpoint URL provided by the Serverless Framework:

```php
Copy code
https://<api-id>.execute-api.<region>.amazonaws.com/dev/hello?name=Alice
```

Replace <api-id> and <region> with the values specific to your deployment. When you access this URL, you should see the following JSON response:

```json
Copy code
{
    "message": "Hello, Alice!"
}
```

If you access the endpoint without the name parameter:

```php
Copy code
https://<api-id>.execute-api.<region>.amazonaws.com/dev/hello
```

You should receive:

```json
Copy code
```

```
{
    "message": "Hello, World!"
}
```

Step 7: Monitoring and Logging

AWS Lambda integrates with Amazon CloudWatch, allowing you to monitor your function's performance and view logs. You can set up alarms for metrics like invocation errors and duration.

To view logs for your deployed function, use the following command:

```bash
Copy code
serverless logs -f hello
```

This command retrieves the logs for the hello function, allowing you to debug any issues or monitor performance.

Step 8: Updating Your Function

As you develop your application, you may want to update your function. Simply modify the code in handler.py and then redeploy your application using:

```bash
Copy code
serverless deploy
```

This command redeploys only the modified functions, ensuring your application remains up-to-date without downtime.

Step 9: Cleaning Up Resources

After testing, it's good practice to clean up your resources to avoid unnecessary charges on your AWS account. You can remove the deployed service by running:

```bash
Copy code
serverless remove
```

This command deletes all resources created during the deployment process.

Hands-On Example: Building a Simple Serverless Function

In this section, we will put together everything we've learned by building a more comprehensive serverless application that includes an AWS Lambda function, an API Gateway trigger, and uses DynamoDB for data storage.

Step 1: Setting Up the Project Structure

Create a new directory for your project and navigate to it:

```bash
Copy code
mkdir serverless-todo-app
cd serverless-todo-app
```

Step 2: Creating the serverless.yml Configuration File

Create a serverless.yml file in the project directory with the following content:

```yaml
yaml
Copy code
service: serverless-todo-app

provider:
  name: aws
  runtime: python3.8
  region: us-east-1

resources:
  Resources:
    TodosTable:
      Type: AWS::DynamoDB::Table
      Properties:
        TableName: Todos
        AttributeDefinitions:
          - AttributeName: id
            AttributeType: S
        KeySchema:
          - AttributeName: id
            KeyType: HASH
        ProvisionedThroughput:
          ReadCapacityUnits: 1
          WriteCapacityUnits: 1

functions:
  createTodo:
    handler: handler.create
    events:
      - http:
          path: todos
          method: post

  getTodos:
    handler: handler.get_all
    events:
      - http:
          path: todos
          method: get
```

In this configuration, we define:

- A DynamoDB table named Todos to store our todo items.
- Two Lambda functions: createTodo for creating todo items and getTodos for retrieving all todo items.

Step 3: Writing the Lambda Functions

Create a handler.py file in your project directory and write the following code:

```python
python
Copy code
import json
import boto3
import uuid

dynamodb = boto3.resource('dynamodb')
table = dynamodb.Table('Todos')

def create(event, context):
    body = json.loads(event['body'])
    todo_id = str(uuid.uuid4())
    todo_item = {
        'id': todo_id,
        'task': body['task'],
        'completed': False
    }

    table.put_item(Item=todo_item)

    return {
        'statusCode': 201,
        'body': json.dumps(todo_item)
    }

def get_all(event, context):
    response = table.scan()
    todos = response.get('Items', [])
```

```
return {
    'statusCode': 200,
    'body': json.dumps(todos)
}
```

In this code:

- The create function generates a unique ID for each todo item and adds it to the DynamoDB table.
- The get_all function retrieves all todo items from the table.

Step 4: Installing Required Dependencies

Since we're using boto3 to interact with DynamoDB, we need to specify it in a requirements.txt file:

```
Copy code
boto3
```

Step 5: Deploying the Application

Deploy your application using the following command:

```bash
Copy code
serverless deploy
```

Once the deployment is complete, you'll receive the endpoints for your createTodo and getTodos functions.

Step 6: Testing the Create Function

You can use a tool like Postman or curl to test the createTodo function. To create a new todo item, send a POST request to the endpoint provided:

```bash
Copy code
curl -X POST
https://<api-id>.execute-api.us-east-1.amazonaws.com/dev/todos -d
'{"task": "Learn Serverless"}'
```

Make sure to replace <api-id> with your specific API ID.

The response should include the created todo item:

```json
Copy code
{
    "id": "some-unique-id",
    "task": "Learn Serverless",
    "completed": false
}
```

Step 7: Testing the Get Function

To retrieve all todo items, send a GET request to the getTodos endpoint:

```bash
Copy code
curl -X GET
https://<api-id>.execute-api.us-east-1.amazonaws.com/dev/todos
```

You should receive a response containing all todo items in the DynamoDB table:

```json
json
Copy code
[
    {
        "id": "some-unique-id",
        "task": "Learn Serverless",
        "completed": false
    }
]
```

Step 8: Monitoring and Logging

You can monitor and log the execution of your functions using the following command:

```bash
bash
Copy code
serverless logs -f createTodo
```

This command retrieves the logs for the createTodo function, allowing you to view execution details and troubleshoot any issues.

Step 9: Cleaning Up Resources

Once you're finished with the example application, remember to clean up resources to avoid unnecessary charges:

```bash
bash
Copy code
serverless remove
```

This command deletes the entire stack, including the DynamoDB table and the Lambda functions.

Conclusion

In this chapter, we explored AWS Lambda in detail, including its key features and the event-driven architecture that underpins it. We learned how to write and deploy Python functions to AWS Lambda, and we built a simple serverless application that interacts with AWS DynamoDB.

AWS Lambda empowers developers to create scalable, cost-effective applications without the overhead of managing infrastructure. By leveraging the Serverless Framework, you can streamline your development workflow, quickly deploy functions, and focus on delivering value to your users.

In the next chapter, we will explore advanced topics such as performance optimization, best practices for developing serverless applications, and additional AWS services that can enhance your serverless architecture.

Chapter 5: Building and Managing APIs with AWS Lambda and API Gateway

I n the world of modern applications, APIs (Application Programming Interfaces) play a crucial role in enabling communication between different components of a system or between various services. AWS Lambda, in conjunction with Amazon API Gateway, provides a powerful solution for building and managing APIs in a serverless architecture. This chapter will delve into the process of creating and deploying APIs using AWS Lambda and API Gateway, focusing on best practices, security considerations, and real-world examples.

Understanding API Gateway

What is Amazon API Gateway?

Amazon API Gateway is a fully managed service that simplifies the creation, deployment, and management of APIs at any scale. It allows developers to create RESTful APIs and WebSocket APIs that can be easily integrated with various backend services, including AWS Lambda, AWS Elastic Beanstalk, and other AWS services.

Key Features of API Gateway

1. **Managed Service**: API Gateway handles the infrastructure management, allowing developers to focus on defining the API endpoints and their integration with backend services.
2. **Support for RESTful and WebSocket APIs**: API Gateway supports both RESTful APIs for traditional HTTP communication and WebSocket APIs for real-time communication.
3. **Integration with AWS Services**: API Gateway seamlessly integrates with AWS Lambda, making it easy to build serverless APIs. It can also integrate with other AWS services, such as DynamoDB, S3, and more.
4. **Security and Access Control**: API Gateway provides robust security features, including API key management, request throttling, and integration with AWS IAM for access control.
5. **Monitoring and Analytics**: API Gateway integrates with Amazon CloudWatch for monitoring and logging, allowing you to track API usage, performance, and errors.
6. **Custom Domain Names**: You can set up custom domain names for your APIs, providing a user-friendly URL structure for your applications.

Why Use API Gateway with AWS Lambda?

Using API Gateway in conjunction with AWS Lambda offers several advantages for building serverless APIs:

- **Cost-Effectiveness**: With API Gateway and Lambda, you only pay for the resources you consume, making it a cost-effective solution for building APIs that may have variable workloads.
- **Scalability**: Both API Gateway and Lambda automatically scale based on demand. This ensures that your API can handle a large number of requests without manual intervention.
- **Reduced Operational Overhead**: API Gateway takes care of managing the underlying infrastructure, allowing developers to focus on building and deploying APIs.

- **Rapid Development**: By leveraging the serverless architecture, developers can quickly prototype, test, and deploy APIs without worrying about server management or capacity planning.

Creating a Serverless API with AWS Lambda and API Gateway

Now that we have a foundational understanding of AWS API Gateway and its integration with AWS Lambda, let's walk through the process of building a simple serverless API. In this example, we will create an API for managing a collection of todo items.

Step 1: Setting Up Your Project Structure

First, create a new directory for your serverless API project:

```bash
Copy code
mkdir serverless-todo-api
cd serverless-todo-api
```

Step 2: Creating the serverless.yml Configuration File

Create a new serverless.yml file in your project directory with the following configuration:

```yaml
Copy code
service: serverless-todo-api

provider:
  name: aws
  runtime: python3.8

functions:
```

```yaml
createTodo:
  handler: handler.create
  events:
    - http:
        path: todos
        method: post

getTodos:
  handler: handler.get_all
  events:
    - http:
        path: todos
        method: get

updateTodo:
  handler: handler.update
  events:
    - http:
        path: todos/{id}
        method: put

deleteTodo:
  handler: handler.delete
  events:
    - http:
        path: todos/{id}
        method: delete

resources:
  Resources:
    TodosTable:
      Type: AWS::DynamoDB::Table
      Properties:
        TableName: Todos
        AttributeDefinitions:
          - AttributeName: id
            AttributeType: S
        KeySchema:
          - AttributeName: id
            KeyType: HASH
```

```
ProvisionedThroughput:
  ReadCapacityUnits: 1
  WriteCapacityUnits: 1
```

In this configuration:

- We define the service name as serverless-todo-api.
- We specify AWS as the provider and set the runtime to Python 3.8.
- We declare four Lambda functions for creating, retrieving, updating, and deleting todo items. Each function is triggered by an HTTP event, and the paths for the update and delete functions include a path parameter ({id}) to specify the todo item.

Step 3: Writing the Lambda Functions

Create a new file named handler.py in your project directory and write the following code:

```python
python
Copy code
import json
import boto3
import uuid

dynamodb = boto3.resource('dynamodb')
table = dynamodb.Table('Todos')

def create(event, context):
    body = json.loads(event['body'])
    todo_id = str(uuid.uuid4())
    todo_item = {
        'id': todo_id,
        'task': body['task'],
        'completed': False
    }
```

```python
    table.put_item(Item=todo_item)

    return {
        'statusCode': 201,
        'body': json.dumps(todo_item)
    }

def get_all(event, context):
    response = table.scan()
    todos = response.get('Items', [])

    return {
        'statusCode': 200,
        'body': json.dumps(todos)
    }

def update(event, context):
    todo_id = event['pathParameters']['id']
    body = json.loads(event['body'])
    completed = body.get('completed')

    table.update_item(
        Key={'id': todo_id},
        UpdateExpression='SET completed = :val',
        ExpressionAttributeValues={':val': completed}
    )

    return {
        'statusCode': 200,
        'body': json.dumps({'id': todo_id, 'completed':
        completed})
    }

def delete(event, context):
    todo_id = event['pathParameters']['id']

    table.delete_item(Key={'id': todo_id})

    return {
        'statusCode': 204
```

```
    }
```

In this code:

- The create function generates a unique ID for each todo item and adds it to the DynamoDB table.
- The get_all function retrieves all todo items from the table.
- The update function updates the completion status of a specific todo item based on the provided ID.
- The delete function deletes a todo item from the table based on the provided ID.

Step 4: Installing Required Dependencies

In this example, we are using the boto3 library to interact with DynamoDB. Create a requirements.txt file in your project directory and include the following:

```
Copy code
boto3
```

Step 5: Deploying the API

Deploy your API using the following command:

```bash
Copy code
serverless deploy
```

Once the deployment is complete, you'll receive the endpoints for your createTodo, getTodos, updateTodo, and deleteTodo functions.

Step 6: Testing the API Endpoints

Now that your API is deployed, let's test the endpoints using a tool like Postman or curl.

Creating a Todo Item

To create a new todo item, send a POST request to the createTodo endpoint:

```bash
Copy code
curl -X POST
https://<api-id>.execute-api.us-east-1.amazonaws.com/dev/todos -d
'{"task": "Learn AWS Lambda"}' -H "Content-Type: application/json"
```

You should receive a response similar to this:

```json
Copy code
{
    "id": "some-unique-id",
    "task": "Learn AWS Lambda",
    "completed": false
}
```

Retrieving All Todo Items

To retrieve all todo items, send a GET request to the getTodos endpoint:

```bash
Copy code
curl -X GET
https://<api-id>.execute-api.us-east-1.amazonaws.com/dev/todos
```

The response should include all todo items in the DynamoDB table:

```json
Copy code
```

```
[
    {
        "id": "some-unique-id",
        "task": "Learn AWS Lambda",
        "completed": false
    }
]
```

Updating a Todo Item

To update the completion status of a todo item, send a PUT request to the updateTodo endpoint, including the ID of the todo item in the URL and the new completion status in the body:

```bash
bash
Copy code
curl -X PUT https://<api-id>.
execute-api.us-east-1.
amazonaws.com/dev/todos/some-unique-
id -d '{"completed": true}'
  -H "Content-Type: application/json"
```

The response should indicate the updated status:

```json
json
Copy code
{
    "id": "some-unique-id",
    "completed": true
}
```

Deleting a Todo Item

To delete a todo item, send a DELETE request to the deleteTodo endpoint, including the ID of the todo item in the URL:

```bash
Copy code
curl -X DELETE https://
<api-id>.execute-api.us-east-1.
amazonaws.com/
dev/todos/some-unique-id
```

You should receive a 204 No Content response, indicating that the item was successfully deleted.

Step 7: Monitoring and Logging

To monitor your API and view logs, you can use the following command:

```bash
Copy code
serverless logs -f createTodo
```

This command retrieves the logs for the createTodo function, allowing you to debug any issues or monitor performance.

Best Practices for Building Serverless APIs

Building serverless APIs with AWS Lambda and API Gateway comes with its own set of best practices that can help you create efficient, scalable, and maintainable applications. Here are some important considerations:

1. Use Environment Variables for Configuration

Instead of hardcoding configuration settings or sensitive information directly in your code, use environment variables to store configuration values, such as API keys, database credentials, and other settings. This approach enhances security and allows for easier updates.

2. Validate Input Data

Always validate incoming data to your API functions. Use libraries like **jsonschema** for JSON validation or implement custom validation logic to ensure that the data meets your application's requirements before processing it.

3. Implement Error Handling

Robust error handling is essential for building resilient APIs. Use try-except blocks to catch exceptions and return appropriate error messages to the client. Consider using a consistent error response format to make it easier for clients to handle errors.

4. Set Up Rate Limiting

API Gateway allows you to set up rate limiting to prevent abuse and ensure fair usage of your API. Configure usage plans to restrict the number of requests per second for different API consumers.

5. Optimize Cold Start Performance

Cold starts can introduce latency when your Lambda function is invoked after being idle. To mitigate this, you can:

- Use provisioned concurrency for critical functions.
- Keep your deployment package small by minimizing dependencies and optimizing code.

6. Monitor API Usage and Performance

Use AWS CloudWatch to monitor API usage and performance metrics. Set up alarms for key metrics such as error rates, response times, and throttling events. Regularly review logs to identify potential issues and optimize performance.

7. Enable CORS for Your API

If your API will be accessed from a web browser, enable Cross-Origin Resource Sharing (CORS) in API Gateway. This allows web applications hosted on different domains to interact with your API securely.

8. Use API Gateway Stages

API Gateway allows you to create different stages (e.g., development, testing, production) for your APIs. Use stages to manage different environments and versioning of your APIs, making it easier to deploy changes without affecting production users.

Conclusion

In this chapter, we explored the powerful combination of AWS Lambda and API Gateway for building serverless APIs. We learned about the key features of API Gateway, the process of creating a serverless API, and best practices for developing robust and efficient APIs.

By leveraging AWS Lambda and API Gateway, you can build scalable, cost-effective APIs that respond to real-time events and enable seamless communication between services. In the next chapter, we will dive into advanced API features, such as authentication, authorization, and security measures for protecting your serverless applications.

Chapter 6: Securing Your Serverless API

I n today's digital landscape, securing applications and APIs is more important than ever. With the rapid adoption of serverless architectures, developers must understand how to protect their applications from various security threats. AWS Lambda and Amazon API Gateway provide a robust framework for building serverless APIs, but it's essential to implement best practices for security and compliance. In this chapter, we will explore the strategies and tools available to secure your serverless APIs effectively.

Understanding API Security

What is API Security?

API security refers to the practices and measures taken to protect APIs from unauthorized access, abuse, and exploitation. Given that APIs serve as the gateways between clients and backend services, they are prime targets for attackers. Effective API security involves various strategies, including authentication, authorization, encryption, and input validation.

Key API Security Concepts

1. **Authentication**: This process verifies the identity of users or systems accessing the API. It ensures that only authorized users can interact with the API.
2. **Authorization**: After authentication, authorization determines what actions a user is permitted to perform. It controls access to specific resources and functionalities within the API.
3. **Data Encryption**: Encrypting data in transit and at rest ensures that sensitive information remains secure. This protects data from eavesdropping and unauthorized access.
4. **Input Validation**: Ensuring that input data is validated and sanitized helps prevent injection attacks and other security vulnerabilities.
5. **Rate Limiting**: Rate limiting controls the number of requests a user or system can make to the API in a given timeframe. This helps mitigate abuse and denial-of-service (DoS) attacks.
6. **Logging and Monitoring**: Implementing robust logging and monitoring allows you to track API usage, detect anomalies, and respond to security incidents promptly.

Common Security Threats to APIs

Understanding potential threats is essential for implementing effective security measures. Here are some common security threats to APIs:

1. **Unauthorized Access**: Attackers may attempt to access your API without proper authentication, exposing sensitive data and functionality.
2. **Injection Attacks**: APIs that do not validate input can be vulnerable to injection attacks, such as SQL injection, where malicious input is executed by the backend database.
3. **Cross-Site Scripting (XSS)**: Attackers may exploit vulnerabilities in APIs that return unvalidated user input, allowing them to execute scripts in the user's browser.

4. **Man-in-the-Middle (MitM) Attacks**: Without proper encryption, data transmitted between clients and APIs can be intercepted, leading to data breaches.

5. **Denial-of-Service (DoS) Attacks**: Attackers may flood your API with requests, overwhelming it and causing service disruptions.

6. **Data Exposure**: Inadequate access control may expose sensitive data to unauthorized users.

Securing Your Serverless API with AWS

Now that we understand the importance of API security and common threats, let's explore specific strategies and tools you can use to secure your serverless APIs built with AWS Lambda and API Gateway.

1. Implementing Authentication

Authentication is the first line of defense for securing your serverless API. AWS offers several methods for implementing authentication:

AWS IAM Roles and Policies

For internal AWS services, you can use AWS Identity and Access Management (IAM) roles and policies to control access to your Lambda functions. By defining IAM roles and permissions, you can restrict which AWS services can invoke your Lambda functions. This is particularly useful for securing your API endpoints from unauthorized access by other AWS services.

Amazon Cognito

Amazon Cognito is a robust user authentication service that enables you to add user sign-up, sign-in, and access control to your APIs. You can create user pools to manage user accounts and authentication flows.

- **Setting Up Amazon Cognito**:

1. Create a user pool in the Amazon Cognito console.
2. Configure the sign-up and sign-in settings according to your applica-

tion's requirements.

3. Use the Cognito User Pool ID and App Client ID in your API Gateway settings to enforce authentication for your API.

- **Using Cognito with API Gateway**: After configuring Cognito, you can set up API Gateway to require Cognito tokens for accessing your endpoints. This ensures that only authenticated users can interact with your API.

OAuth 2.0 and OpenID Connect

If your application requires integration with third-party identity providers (IdPs), consider using OAuth 2.0 and OpenID Connect for authentication. AWS API Gateway supports these protocols, allowing you to use popular IdPs like Google, Facebook, or Microsoft Azure for authentication.

2. Implementing Authorization

Authorization determines what authenticated users can do with your API. After ensuring that users are authenticated, you need to control their access to specific resources and actions.

IAM Policies for Resource Access

In AWS, you can define IAM policies that specify the actions a user or role can perform on particular resources. For example, you can create a policy that allows users to invoke specific Lambda functions or access specific DynamoDB tables based on their roles.

Cognito Groups and Roles

With Amazon Cognito, you can create groups to manage user roles and permissions. Users can be assigned to specific groups, each of which can have its own set of permissions. This makes it easier to manage access for different types of users within your application.

API Gateway Resource Policies

API Gateway supports resource policies that allow you to control access to your API based on specific conditions. You can specify which IAM roles or users are allowed to invoke your API methods, ensuring that only authorized users can access sensitive endpoints.

3. Securing Data with Encryption

Data security is critical for protecting sensitive information transmitted between clients and your API. AWS provides several options for securing data:

SSL/TLS Encryption

API Gateway automatically provides SSL/TLS encryption for data in transit. This means that all requests to your API are encrypted, preventing eavesdropping and man-in-the-middle attacks.

- **Enforcing HTTPS**: When you create an API in API Gateway, it is accessible over HTTPS by default. Make sure to enforce HTTPS by not allowing HTTP access to your API endpoints.

Encrypting Data at Rest

For sensitive data stored in services like DynamoDB, S3, or RDS, enable encryption at rest. AWS provides built-in encryption capabilities that can be configured easily:

- **DynamoDB**: Enable encryption at rest for your DynamoDB tables to protect stored data.
- **S3**: Use server-side encryption with S3-managed keys (SSE-S3) or AWS Key Management Service (SSE-KMS) for encrypting files stored in S3.
- **RDS**: Enable encryption for RDS instances during creation to secure data at rest.

4. Input Validation and Data Sanitization

Input validation is crucial for preventing injection attacks and ensuring that only valid data is processed by your API. Always validate and sanitize input data received by your Lambda functions.

Using JSON Schema for Validation

You can use JSON Schema to define the structure and validation rules for incoming JSON data. By implementing input validation in your Lambda functions, you can catch invalid data early and return appropriate error messages.

Here's an example of validating input using JSON Schema:

```python
Copy code
from jsonschema import validate, ValidationError

todo_schema = {
    "type": "object",
    "properties": {
        "task": {"type": "string"},
    },
    "required": ["task"],
}

def create(event, context):
    try:
        body = json.loads(event['body'])
        validate(instance=body, schema=todo_schema)
        # Proceed with creating the todo item
    except ValidationError as e:
        return {
            'statusCode': 400,
            'body': json.dumps({'error': str(e)})
        }
```

5. Rate Limiting and Throttling

Implementing rate limiting is essential for protecting your API from abuse and denial-of-service (DoS) attacks. AWS API Gateway provides built-in support for throttling requests to your API.

Setting Up Throttling in API Gateway

You can configure usage plans in API Gateway that specify the maximum number of requests allowed per second for different API consumers. By enforcing rate limits, you can prevent a single user from overwhelming your API and ensure fair usage for all consumers.

1. **Create a Usage Plan**: In the API Gateway console, create a usage plan and specify the request limits.
2. **Associate API Stages**: Link the usage plan to specific API stages (e.g., development, production).
3. **Distribute API Keys**: Assign API keys to consumers, allowing you to track their usage and apply rate limits accordingly.

6. Logging and Monitoring

Implementing logging and monitoring is crucial for maintaining the security and performance of your serverless APIs. AWS provides several tools for monitoring your Lambda functions and API Gateway.

Using AWS CloudWatch

AWS CloudWatch integrates seamlessly with Lambda and API Gateway, allowing you to monitor metrics, logs, and alarms.

- **Logs**: By default, Lambda functions log output to CloudWatch Logs. You can use the print statements in your functions to log important information or errors.
- **Metrics**: CloudWatch provides built-in metrics for your Lambda functions, including invocation count, error count, and duration. You can set up alarms based on these metrics to be notified of potential issues.

- **Custom Metrics**: You can create custom metrics for your application by publishing data to CloudWatch, allowing you to monitor specific aspects of your API's performance.

7. Securing the API Gateway Endpoint

Beyond securing individual Lambda functions, it's essential to secure the API Gateway endpoint itself. Here are some strategies:

API Key Requirement

You can configure API Gateway to require API keys for accessing your API. This adds an additional layer of security, allowing you to track usage and manage access.

1. **Enable API Key Requirement**: In the API Gateway console, enable the API key requirement for specific methods.
2. **Distribute API Keys**: Create and distribute API keys to authorized consumers of your API.

CORS Configuration

If your API will be accessed from web browsers, ensure that Cross-Origin Resource Sharing (CORS) is configured properly in API Gateway. This prevents unauthorized domains from making requests to your API.

1. **Enable CORS**: In the API Gateway console, enable CORS for the relevant API methods.
2. **Specify Allowed Origins**: Configure the allowed origins and HTTP methods to control which clients can access your API.

8. Regular Security Audits

Conducting regular security audits of your serverless API is essential for identifying and addressing vulnerabilities. Consider the following practices:

- **Review IAM Policies**: Regularly review your IAM policies to ensure they follow the principle of least privilege.
- **Penetration Testing**: Conduct penetration testing to identify potential vulnerabilities in your API and infrastructure.
- **Compliance Checks**: Ensure that your API meets relevant compliance requirements, such as GDPR, HIPAA, or PCI-DSS.

Conclusion

In this chapter, we explored the critical aspects of securing your serverless API built with AWS Lambda and API Gateway. We discussed various strategies for implementing authentication and authorization, encrypting data, validating input, and enforcing rate limits. Additionally, we covered the importance of logging and monitoring, securing the API Gateway endpoint, and conducting regular security audits.

By following these best practices and leveraging the security features provided by AWS, you can build robust, secure serverless APIs that protect sensitive data and ensure reliable performance. In the next chapter, we will explore advanced serverless architectures, including event-driven workflows, orchestration, and integrating with other AWS services to create powerful, scalable applications.

Chapter 7: Monitoring and Logging in Serverless Applications

A s applications become increasingly complex, monitoring and logging have become essential for ensuring reliability, performance, and security. In serverless architectures, where components may scale dynamically and run in ephemeral environments, effective monitoring and logging are crucial for gaining visibility into application behavior and troubleshooting issues. In this chapter, we will explore the monitoring and logging capabilities available in AWS Lambda and API Gateway, as well as best practices for implementing these capabilities in your serverless applications.

Understanding the Importance of Monitoring and Logging

What is Monitoring?

Monitoring refers to the continuous observation of application performance and behavior to ensure that it meets established service-level agreements (SLAs) and operates efficiently. In the context of serverless applications, monitoring involves tracking metrics such as execution time, error rates, and request counts to gain insights into application performance.

What is Logging?

Logging is the process of recording information about application events, errors, and transactions in a structured format. Logs are critical for debugging and troubleshooting, as they provide detailed information about application behavior and can help identify the root causes of issues.

Why Are Monitoring and Logging Essential in Serverless Architectures?

1. **Visibility**: Serverless applications may involve multiple services and functions that communicate asynchronously. Monitoring and logging provide visibility into the interactions between these components, helping developers understand application behavior.
2. **Debugging**: When issues arise in serverless applications, logs provide essential information for diagnosing problems. Without adequate logging, it can be challenging to trace errors or understand the context of a failure.
3. **Performance Optimization**: Monitoring allows you to track performance metrics and identify bottlenecks or areas for improvement. By analyzing execution times and resource usage, you can optimize your serverless functions for better performance.
4. **Cost Management**: Monitoring usage patterns helps you manage costs by identifying underutilized functions or unexpected spikes in usage that may lead to increased expenses.
5. **Security Auditing**: Logs can be used for security audits, providing a record of API access and interactions. This is crucial for identifying unauthorized access or suspicious activity.

Monitoring AWS Lambda Functions

AWS Lambda integrates seamlessly with Amazon CloudWatch, allowing you to monitor the performance of your Lambda functions in real time. CloudWatch provides built-in metrics and dashboards that enable you to gain insights into your serverless applications.

Key Metrics for Monitoring AWS Lambda

1. **Invocation Count**: This metric shows the total number of times your Lambda function has been invoked. Monitoring invocation counts helps you understand usage patterns and identify trends.
2. **Duration**: The duration metric indicates how long your Lambda function takes to execute. Monitoring execution times allows you to identify performance bottlenecks and optimize your code.
3. **Error Count**: This metric tracks the number of errors encountered during function execution. Monitoring error rates is essential for identifying issues that may affect application reliability.
4. **Throttles**: This metric indicates the number of times a function invocation is throttled due to reaching concurrency limits. Monitoring throttles helps you understand whether your application can handle traffic spikes.
5. **Cold Start Duration**: For functions that experience cold starts, this metric tracks the time taken to initialize a function before processing requests. Monitoring cold start durations can help you optimize function performance.

Setting Up CloudWatch Alarms

AWS CloudWatch allows you to set up alarms based on specific metrics. Alarms can notify you when metrics exceed defined thresholds, enabling you to take proactive action. For example, you can set up alarms for high error rates or increased execution duration.

1. **Creating an Alarm**:

- Navigate to the CloudWatch console in the AWS Management Console.
- Select "Alarms" and click "Create Alarm."
- Choose the Lambda function metric you want to monitor (e.g., "Errors").
- Define the threshold for the alarm (e.g., if errors exceed a certain number).
- Configure notifications (e.g., sending an email or triggering an SNS topic).

Creating Custom Metrics

In addition to the built-in metrics provided by CloudWatch, you can create custom metrics for your Lambda functions. Custom metrics allow you to track specific application behavior or business KPIs that are relevant to your use case.

To publish custom metrics, use the put_metric_data API provided by Boto3:

```python
Copy code
import boto3

cloudwatch = boto3.client('cloudwatch')

def publish_custom_metric(value):
    cloudwatch.put_metric_data(
        Namespace='MyApp',
        MetricData=[
            {
                'MetricName': 'MyCustomMetric',
                'Value': value,
                'Unit': 'Count'
            },
        ]
    )
```

In this example, the publish_custom_metric function publishes a custom metric named MyCustomMetric to CloudWatch, allowing you to track specific application events.

Logging AWS Lambda Functions

Effective logging is crucial for understanding the behavior of your AWS Lambda functions. AWS Lambda automatically captures logs for your functions and sends them to Amazon CloudWatch Logs, where you can view and analyze them.

Viewing Logs in CloudWatch

To view logs for a specific Lambda function:

1. Navigate to the AWS Lambda console.
2. Select your Lambda function.
3. Click on the "Monitor" tab.
4. Under "View logs in CloudWatch," click the link to open CloudWatch Logs.

You can also view logs directly in the CloudWatch console:

1. Navigate to the CloudWatch console.
2. Select "Logs" from the sidebar.
3. Choose the log group for your Lambda function (named /aws/lambda/ <function-name>).
4. Click on the desired log stream to view log entries.

Structured Logging

While AWS Lambda logs are useful, structured logging provides more context and makes it easier to parse logs for specific information. Structured logs are typically formatted as JSON, allowing you to include key-value pairs that provide insights into application behavior.

Here's an example of structured logging in Python:

```python
Copy code
import json
import logging

logger = logging.getLogger()
logger.setLevel(logging.INFO)

def lambda_handler(event, context):
    logger.info(json.dumps({
        'event': event,
        'context': context,
        'message': 'Function executed successfully'
    }))
```

In this example, the log entry contains the event data, context information, and a custom message, all formatted as a JSON object.

Centralized Logging with AWS CloudWatch Logs Insights

AWS CloudWatch Logs Insights provides a powerful query capability for analyzing log data. With CloudWatch Logs Insights, you can run queries against your logs to extract insights, visualize data, and troubleshoot issues more effectively.

1. **Accessing Logs Insights**:

- Navigate to the CloudWatch console.

- Select "Logs Insights" from the sidebar.
- Choose the log group for your Lambda function.

1. **Running Queries**: You can write queries using the CloudWatch Logs Insights query syntax. For example, to count the number of log entries with errors, you can use the following query:

```sql
Copy code
fields @timestamp, @message
| filter @message like /ERROR/
| stats count(*) as errorCount
| sort @timestamp desc
```

1. This query filters log entries for messages containing "ERROR" and counts the occurrences, providing insights into error rates.

Best Practices for Monitoring and Logging in Serverless Applications

To ensure effective monitoring and logging in your serverless applications, consider the following best practices:

1. Establish Clear Logging Standards

Define a consistent logging strategy across your Lambda functions. Establish standards for log levels (e.g., DEBUG, INFO, ERROR) and use structured logging to include relevant context. This consistency will make it easier to analyze logs across multiple functions.

2. Monitor Key Metrics Regularly

Set up CloudWatch dashboards to visualize key metrics for your Lambda functions and API Gateway endpoints. Monitor metrics such as invocation count, error rates, and duration to identify trends and anomalies.

3. Implement Alerts for Critical Issues

Configure CloudWatch alarms for critical metrics, such as high error rates or excessive execution duration. Set up notifications to alert your team when alarms are triggered, allowing for timely investigation and resolution.

4. Optimize Log Retention Policies

AWS CloudWatch Logs charges based on the volume of log data stored. Implement log retention policies to automatically delete old logs after a certain period. This helps manage costs while retaining logs for necessary troubleshooting.

5. Use Structured Logs for Better Analysis

Utilize structured logging formats (e.g., JSON) to facilitate easier log parsing and analysis. Structured logs can be indexed and searched more effectively, making it easier to extract insights.

6. Leverage Third-Party Logging Solutions

Consider integrating third-party logging solutions (e.g., ELK Stack, Datadog, Splunk) for more advanced log analysis and visualization capabilities. These tools can provide enhanced features for monitoring and troubleshooting serverless applications.

7. Regularly Review and Audit Logs

Schedule regular audits of your logs to identify any security incidents or anomalies. This proactive approach helps ensure that potential issues are addressed before they escalate.

8. Integrate Monitoring into Development Workflow

Incorporate monitoring and logging into your development workflow. Ensure that new features and changes include appropriate logging and monitoring to facilitate ongoing visibility.

Conclusion

In this chapter, we explored the critical role of monitoring and logging in serverless applications, specifically focusing on AWS Lambda and API Gateway. We discussed the importance of monitoring key metrics, implementing effective logging strategies, and leveraging AWS CloudWatch for insights into application performance.

By following best practices for monitoring and logging, you can ensure the reliability, security, and performance of your serverless applications. In the next chapter, we will dive into advanced topics, including implementing CI/CD (Continuous Integration and Continuous Deployment) pipelines for serverless applications and strategies for automating deployment and testing.

Chapter 8: Implementing CI/CD for Serverless Applications

C ontinuous Integration (CI) and Continuous Deployment (CD) have become essential practices in modern software development, enabling teams to deliver high-quality software at a faster pace. In the context of serverless applications, CI/CD processes streamline development, testing, and deployment, ensuring that new features and bug fixes reach users quickly and reliably. This chapter will explore the principles of CI/CD, tools and best practices for implementing CI/CD in serverless applications, and a step-by-step guide to setting up a CI/CD pipeline for an AWS Lambda application.

Understanding CI/CD in the Context of Serverless

What is CI/CD?

- **Continuous Integration (CI)**: CI is the practice of automatically testing and integrating code changes into a shared repository. Developers frequently commit code to the repository, and automated tests run to ensure that new changes do not break existing functionality. This process helps detect bugs early, improves code quality, and enhances collaboration among team members.

- **Continuous Deployment (CD)**: CD is the practice of automatically deploying code changes to production after passing the CI pipeline. This enables rapid delivery of new features and bug fixes to users without manual intervention. In a serverless context, CD often involves deploying updates to AWS Lambda functions, API Gateway configurations, and related resources.

Benefits of Implementing CI/CD for Serverless Applications

1. **Faster Development Cycles**: By automating testing and deployment, CI/CD reduces the time required to deliver new features and fixes, allowing teams to respond to user feedback quickly.
2. **Improved Code Quality**: Automated testing ensures that code changes are validated before deployment, helping to catch bugs early and maintain high code quality.
3. **Reduced Manual Errors**: Automation minimizes the risk of human error during the deployment process, leading to more reliable releases.
4. **Consistent Deployment**: CI/CD pipelines provide a standardized process for deploying serverless applications, ensuring consistency across different environments (development, staging, production).
5. **Enhanced Collaboration**: CI/CD promotes collaboration among development, testing, and operations teams by providing a shared framework for managing code changes and deployments.

Key Components of a CI/CD Pipeline for Serverless Applications

A CI/CD pipeline for serverless applications typically consists of several stages, each with specific tasks and objectives. Here are the key components of a CI/CD pipeline:

1. Source Control Management

The pipeline begins with source control management, where developers commit their code changes to a version control system (VCS) such as Git. A popular choice is to use platforms like GitHub, GitLab, or Bitbucket to host the repository.

2. Automated Testing

Once code changes are pushed to the repository, automated tests run to validate the functionality of the application. This may include:

- **Unit Tests**: Test individual functions or components to ensure they work as expected.
- **Integration Tests**: Test the interaction between different components or services.
- **End-to-End Tests**: Simulate real user scenarios to validate the entire application flow.

3. Build Stage

In the build stage, the application is packaged and prepared for deployment. This includes installing dependencies, compiling code (if necessary), and generating deployment artifacts. For serverless applications, this often involves creating a deployment package for AWS Lambda functions and configuring infrastructure as code (IaC) definitions.

4. Deployment

The deployment stage involves deploying the application to a specified environment (e.g., development, staging, production). This can include:

- Deploying Lambda functions and associated resources (e.g., API Gateway,

DynamoDB) using IaC tools like AWS CloudFormation or the Serverless Framework.

- Running database migrations or other setup tasks as part of the deployment process.

5. Monitoring and Feedback

After deployment, monitoring tools track the performance and health of the application in production. This stage allows teams to gather feedback from users, identify issues, and respond to incidents quickly. Monitoring tools can include AWS CloudWatch, AWS X-Ray, and third-party solutions like Datadog or New Relic.

6. Rollback Mechanisms

In the event of a failure or critical issue in production, having a rollback mechanism in place allows teams to revert to a previous stable version of the application quickly. This can be achieved through versioning of Lambda functions or by using deployment tools that support rollback functionality.

Tools for Implementing CI/CD in Serverless Applications

Several tools can help automate the CI/CD process for serverless applications. Below are some popular options:

1. AWS CodePipeline

AWS CodePipeline is a fully managed CI/CD service that automates the build, test, and deployment phases of your application. It integrates with other AWS services such as CodeBuild, CodeDeploy, and Lambda, making it an ideal choice for serverless applications.

- **Key Features**:

- Visual interface for designing your CI/CD pipeline.
- Integration with Git-based repositories for source control.
- Support for custom actions and third-party integrations.

2. AWS CodeBuild

AWS CodeBuild is a fully managed build service that compiles source code, runs tests, and produces deployment artifacts. It can be used in conjunction with AWS CodePipeline to automate the build process for your serverless application.

- **Key Features**:
- Customizable build environments using Docker images.
- Automatic scaling to handle concurrent builds.
- Integration with AWS services for streamlined workflows.

3. AWS SAM (Serverless Application Model)

AWS SAM is an open-source framework for building serverless applications on AWS. It simplifies the deployment process by providing a syntax for defining serverless resources and a CLI for building and deploying applications.

- **Key Features**:
- Built-in support for local testing and debugging.
- Integration with AWS CloudFormation for infrastructure as code.
- Simplified configuration for AWS Lambda functions and API Gateway.

4. Serverless Framework

The Serverless Framework is a popular open-source framework for building serverless applications. It allows developers to define their serverless architecture using a configuration file (serverless.yml) and provides commands for deploying applications to AWS.

- **Key Features**:
- Multi-cloud support for deploying serverless applications to various providers.
- Plugin ecosystem for extending functionality.
- Built-in support for managing functions, events, and resources.

5. GitHub Actions

GitHub Actions is a CI/CD solution built into GitHub that enables developers to automate workflows directly from their GitHub repositories. You can create custom workflows to build, test, and deploy serverless applications whenever code changes are made.

- **Key Features**:
- Integration with GitHub repositories for seamless automation.
- Support for various event triggers, including pull requests and commits.
- A rich marketplace of pre-built actions for common tasks.

Setting Up a CI/CD Pipeline for AWS Lambda

Now that we have covered the tools available for CI/CD, let's walk through the process of setting up a CI/CD pipeline for an AWS Lambda application using the Serverless Framework and GitHub Actions.

Step 1: Create Your Serverless Application

Start by creating a new serverless application using the Serverless Framework:

```bash
Copy code
mkdir my-serverless-app
cd my-serverless-app
```

```
serverless create --template aws-python --path .
```

This command will generate a basic serverless application structure.

Step 2: Define Your Application

Edit the serverless.yml file to define your Lambda function and API Gateway configuration. For example:

```yaml
yaml
Copy code
service: my-serverless-app

provider:
  name: aws
  runtime: python3.8

functions:
  hello:
    handler: handler.hello
    events:
      - http:
          path: hello
          method: get
```

Step 3: Write Your Lambda Function

Open the handler.py file and implement a simple Lambda function:

```python
python
Copy code
def hello(event, context):
    return {
        "statusCode": 200,
        "body": "Hello, Serverless!"
```

```
}
```

Step 4: Set Up GitHub Repository

1. Initialize a Git repository in your project directory:

```bash
Copy code
git init
git add .
git commit -m "Initial commit"
```

1. Create a new repository on GitHub and push your code:

```bash
Copy code
git remote add origin
https://github.com/yourusername/my-serverless-app.git
git push -u origin master
```

Step 5: Create GitHub Actions Workflow

Create a new directory in your project named .github/workflows and add a file called ci-cd.yml. This file will define your CI/CD workflow:

```yaml
Copy code
name: CI/CD Pipeline

on:
```

```yaml
push:
  branches:
    - master

jobs:
  build:
    runs-on: ubuntu-latest

    steps:
      - name: Checkout code
        uses: actions/checkout@v2

      - name: Set up Python
        uses: actions/setup-python@v2
        with:
          python-version: '3.8'

      - name: Install dependencies
        run: |
          pip install serverless

      - name: Deploy to AWS
        run: |
          serverless deploy --stage prod --region us-east-1
        env:
          AWS_ACCESS_KEY_ID: ${{ secrets.AWS_ACCESS_KEY_ID }}
          AWS_SECRET_ACCESS_KEY: ${{
          secrets.AWS_SECRET_ACCESS_KEY }}
```

In this workflow:

- The workflow is triggered on every push to the master branch.
- It checks out the code, sets up Python, installs the Serverless Framework, and deploys the application to AWS.
- AWS credentials are retrieved from GitHub Secrets, ensuring sensitive information is kept secure.

Step 6: Configure GitHub Secrets

To securely store your AWS credentials, navigate to your GitHub repository settings:

1. Go to the "Secrets" section.
2. Click on "New repository secret."
3. Add the following secrets:

- AWS_ACCESS_KEY_ID: Your AWS Access Key ID.
- AWS_SECRET_ACCESS_KEY: Your AWS Secret Access Key.

Step 7: Push Changes and Trigger Deployment

After configuring the GitHub Actions workflow and secrets, commit the changes to your repository:

```bash
Copy code
git add .
git commit -m "Set up CI/CD pipeline"
git push origin master
```

This action will trigger the CI/CD workflow, automatically deploying your serverless application to AWS.

Step 8: Monitoring the Deployment

You can monitor the status of your deployment in the "Actions" tab of your GitHub repository. Here, you can see the progress of each step in the workflow. If any step fails, you can click on it to view logs and troubleshoot issues.

Best Practices for CI/CD in Serverless Applications

To ensure a successful CI/CD implementation for your serverless applications, consider the following best practices:

1. Keep Your Pipeline Simple

Avoid overcomplicating your CI/CD pipeline. Start with a straightforward setup that includes essential steps for building, testing, and deploying your application. As your application evolves, you can gradually enhance the pipeline with additional features.

2. Automate Testing

Incorporate automated testing into your CI/CD pipeline to validate code changes. Use unit tests, integration tests, and end-to-end tests to ensure the reliability of your application before deployment.

3. Implement Versioning

Versioning your Lambda functions allows you to manage deployments and rollbacks effectively. Each deployment should create a new version of the Lambda function, enabling you to revert to a previous version if needed.

4. Use Infrastructure as Code (IaC)

Leverage Infrastructure as Code tools, such as AWS CloudFormation or the Serverless Framework, to define and manage your serverless resources. This approach ensures that your infrastructure is versioned alongside your application code.

5. Monitor Performance and Usage

Implement monitoring and logging to track the performance and usage of your serverless applications. Use tools like AWS CloudWatch to set up alarms and gather metrics for proactive management.

6. Secure Your CI/CD Pipeline

Ensure that your CI/CD pipeline is secure by using GitHub Secrets to manage sensitive information, implementing access controls, and regularly reviewing your security posture.

7. Foster Collaboration

Encourage collaboration between development, operations, and security teams. CI/CD is most effective when everyone involved in the development lifecycle works together to ensure high-quality software delivery.

Conclusion

In this chapter, we explored the principles of Continuous Integration and Continuous Deployment (CI/CD) and their importance in the development of serverless applications. We discussed the key components of a CI/CD pipeline and the tools available for automating the process.

By following best practices for implementing CI/CD in serverless applications, you can ensure rapid delivery of high-quality software while maintaining reliability and security. In the next chapter, we will delve into advanced topics, including integrating serverless applications with other AWS services and building event-driven architectures to enhance scalability and responsiveness.

Chapter 9: Event-Driven Architectures in Serverless Applications

E vent-driven architectures have emerged as a powerful paradigm for building applications that are scalable, responsive, and resilient. In serverless computing, event-driven architectures leverage the capabilities of AWS Lambda and other cloud services to react to events in real time, enabling developers to create highly efficient applications. This chapter explores the principles of event-driven architectures, how they integrate with serverless applications, and practical examples of building event-driven workflows using AWS services.

Understanding Event-Driven Architectures

What is an Event-Driven Architecture?

An event-driven architecture (EDA) is a software design pattern in which components of a system communicate with one another through the production and consumption of events. Events represent significant changes in the state of a system or external occurrences that trigger actions. In an EDA, components react to events as they occur, promoting a decoupled and asynchronous communication model.

Key Concepts of Event-Driven Architectures

1. **Event Producers**: These are components that generate events based on specific actions or changes in state. For example, an API that processes user sign-ups can produce an event when a new user registers.
2. **Event Consumers**: Event consumers are components that listen for and respond to events. In a serverless context, AWS Lambda functions often serve as event consumers that execute code in response to specific events.
3. **Event Brokers**: An event broker is an intermediary that facilitates the communication between event producers and consumers. It decouples the components by allowing them to interact without knowing about each other's existence. AWS services such as Amazon SNS (Simple Notification Service) and Amazon EventBridge can act as event brokers.
4. **Event Types**: Events can be categorized into different types based on their purpose. Common types include state change events (e.g., a record is created or updated), action events (e.g., a user performs an action), and notification events (e.g., system alerts).

Benefits of Event-Driven Architectures

1. **Scalability**: Event-driven architectures naturally scale as new events can trigger additional processing without modifying existing components. This makes it easy to handle varying workloads.
2. **Decoupling**: By separating event producers and consumers, event-driven architectures promote loose coupling between components. This enables teams to develop, deploy, and maintain components independently.
3. **Flexibility**: Event-driven architectures allow for easy addition or removal of components. New consumers can be added to react to existing events without impacting the producers.
4. **Real-Time Processing**: EDAs enable real-time processing of events, making them ideal for applications that require immediate responses, such as chat applications or financial transaction processing.
5. **Resilience**: By decoupling components, event-driven architectures

enhance the resilience of applications. If one component fails, it does not necessarily impact the entire system.

Event-Driven Architectures in Serverless Applications

AWS Lambda is a natural fit for implementing event-driven architectures in serverless applications. Lambda functions can be triggered by various AWS services and events, allowing you to create responsive and scalable applications.

Common Event Sources for AWS Lambda

1. **Amazon S3**: You can trigger Lambda functions in response to events such as file uploads, deletions, or updates in Amazon S3 buckets. This is useful for scenarios like image processing or data analysis.
2. **Amazon DynamoDB Streams**: DynamoDB Streams capture changes to items in a DynamoDB table. You can configure Lambda functions to respond to these changes, allowing you to react to updates in real time.
3. **Amazon SNS**: Amazon Simple Notification Service (SNS) allows you to send messages to multiple subscribers. You can configure SNS topics to trigger Lambda functions when messages are published.
4. **Amazon EventBridge**: EventBridge is a serverless event bus that allows you to connect applications using events. You can create rules that route events from various sources to Lambda functions, enabling complex event-driven workflows.
5. **API Gateway**: When using AWS API Gateway, HTTP requests can trigger Lambda functions, allowing you to build RESTful APIs that react to incoming requests.

Building Event-Driven Workflows with AWS Lambda

Now that we understand the fundamentals of event-driven architectures, let's explore how to build event-driven workflows using AWS Lambda and other AWS services.

Step 1: Setting Up Your AWS Environment

To begin, ensure you have an AWS account set up and the necessary permissions to create AWS Lambda functions, DynamoDB tables, and other services. If you haven't already, install the AWS CLI and configure it with your credentials.

Step 2: Create a DynamoDB Table

For our example, we will create a DynamoDB table that will store todo items. Use the AWS Management Console or AWS CLI to create a table named Todos with the following attributes:

- **Table Name**: Todos
- **Primary Key**: id (String)

You can create the table using the AWS CLI with the following command:

```bash
Copy code
aws dynamodb create-table \
    --table-name Todos \
    --attribute-definitions \
        AttributeName=id,AttributeType=S \
    --key-schema \
        AttributeName=id,KeyType=HASH \
    --provisioned-throughput \
        ReadCapacityUnits=5,WriteCapacityUnits=5
```

Step 3: Create a Lambda Function for CRUD Operations

Next, we will create a Lambda function that will perform CRUD (Create, Read, Update, Delete) operations on the DynamoDB table. Create a new directory for your Lambda function and create a file named handler.py:

```bash
Copy code
mkdir todo-lambda
cd todo-lambda
touch handler.py
```

Open handler.py and write the following code:

```python
Copy code
import json
import boto3
import uuid

dynamodb = boto3.resource('dynamodb')
table = dynamodb.Table('Todos')

def create(event, context):
    body = json.loads(event['body'])
    todo_id = str(uuid.uuid4())
    todo_item = {
        'id': todo_id,
        'task': body['task'],
        'completed': False
    }

    table.put_item(Item=todo_item)

    return {
        'statusCode': 201,
        'body': json.dumps(todo_item)
    }
```

```python
def get_all(event, context):
    response = table.scan()
    todos = response.get('Items', [])

    return {
        'statusCode': 200,
        'body': json.dumps(todos)
    }

def update(event, context):
    todo_id = event['pathParameters']['id']
    body = json.loads(event['body'])
    completed = body.get('completed')

    table.update_item(
        Key={'id': todo_id},
        UpdateExpression='SET completed = :val',
        ExpressionAttributeValues={':val': completed}
    )

    return {
        'statusCode': 200,
        'body': json.dumps({'id': todo_id,
'completed': completed})
    }

def delete(event, context):
    todo_id = event['pathParameters']['id']

    table.delete_item(Key={'id': todo_id})

    return {
        'statusCode': 204
    }
```

This Lambda function provides endpoints for creating, retrieving, updating, and deleting todo items stored in the DynamoDB table.

Step 4: Create the serverless.yml Configuration File

Now, create a serverless.yml file in the todo-lambda directory to define your Lambda function and API Gateway configuration:

```yaml
Copy code
service: todo-lambda

provider:
  name: aws
  runtime: python3.8

functions:
  create:
    handler: handler.create
    events:
      - http:
          path: todos
          method: post

  get_all:
    handler: handler.get_all
    events:
      - http:
          path: todos
          method: get

  update:
    handler: handler.update
    events:
      - http:
          path: todos/{id}
          method: put

  delete:
    handler: handler.delete
    events:
      - http:
```

```
      path: todos/{id}
      method: delete

resources:
  Resources:
    TodosTable:
      Type: AWS::DynamoDB::Table
      Properties:
        TableName: Todos
        AttributeDefinitions:
          - AttributeName: id
            AttributeType: S
        KeySchema:
          - AttributeName: id
            KeyType: HASH
        ProvisionedThroughput:
          ReadCapacityUnits: 1
          WriteCapacityUnits: 1
```

Step 5: Deploy the Serverless Application

Before deploying your application, make sure you have the Serverless Framework installed. If you haven't done so yet, install it using npm:

```bash
Copy code
npm install -g serverless
```

Next, deploy your application using the Serverless Framework:

```bash
Copy code
serverless deploy
```

Once the deployment is complete, you will receive the endpoints for your

CRUD operations.

Step 6: Testing the API Endpoints

Use a tool like Postman or curl to test your API endpoints.

Creating a Todo Item

To create a new todo item, send a POST request to the create endpoint:

```bash
Copy code
curl -X POST https://<api-id>
.execute-api.us-east-1.
amazonaws.com/dev/todos -d
'{"task": "Learn Event-Driven
 Architecture"}' -H "Content-Type:
application/json"
```

You should receive a response similar to this:

```json
Copy code
{
    "id": "some-unique-id",
    "task": "Learn Event-Driven
Architecture",
    "completed": false
}
```

Retrieving All Todo Items

To retrieve all todo items, send a GET request to the get_all endpoint:

```bash
Copy code
curl -X GET https://<api-id>.
execute-api.us-east-1.
amazonaws.com/dev/todos
```

The response should include all todo items in the DynamoDB table:

```json
Copy code
[
    {
        "id": "some-unique-id",
        "task": "Learn Event-Driven Architecture",
        "completed": false
    }
]
```

Updating a Todo Item

To update the completion status of a todo item, send a PUT request to the update endpoint:

```bash
Copy code
curl -X PUT https://<api-id>.
execute-api.us-east-1.
amazonaws.com/dev/todos/
some-unique-id -d
'{"completed": true}' -H
"Content-Type: application/json"
```

You should receive a response indicating the updated status:

```json
Copy code
{
    "id": "some-unique-id",
    "completed": true
}
```

Deleting a Todo Item

To delete a todo item, send a DELETE request to the delete endpoint:

```
bash
Copy code
curl -X DELETE https://
<api-id>.execute-api.us-east-1.
amazonaws.com/dev
/todos/some-unique-id
```

You should receive a 204 No Content response, indicating that the item was successfully deleted.

Building Event-Driven Workflows with AWS Services

Now that we have set up a basic event-driven architecture with CRUD operations, let's explore how to enhance this architecture by integrating other AWS services. We will add an event-driven workflow that triggers additional processing when a new todo item is created.

Step 1: Integrate Amazon SNS

In this example, we will use Amazon Simple Notification Service (SNS) to send notifications whenever a new todo item is created. This could be useful for sending alerts or updating other systems.

Create an SNS Topic

1. Navigate to the Amazon SNS console.
2. Click on "Topics" and then "Create topic."
3. Choose "Standard" for the topic type, enter a name (e.g., TodoNotifications), and click "Create topic."

Add Permissions to Lambda Function

To allow your Lambda function to publish messages to the SNS topic, you need to add the necessary permissions. Update the serverless.yml file to include the following IAM policy under the provider section:

```yaml
Copy code
provider:
  name: aws
  runtime: python3.8
  iamRoleStatements:
    - Effect: Allow
      Action:
        - sns:Publish
      Resource:
        arn:aws:sns:us-east-1:your-account-id:TodoNotifications
```

Step 2: Modify the Create Function

Next, modify the create function to publish a message to the SNS topic when a new todo item is created. Update the handler.py file as follows:

```python
Copy code
import json
import boto3
import uuid

dynamodb = boto3.resource('dynamodb')
sns = boto3.client('sns')
table = dynamodb.Table('Todos')

def create(event, context):
    body = json.loads(event['body'])
    todo_id = str(uuid.uuid4())
    todo_item = {
        'id': todo_id,
        'task': body['task'],
        'completed': False
    }

    table.put_item(Item=todo_item)
```

```
# Publish a message to SNS
sns.publish(
    TopicArn='arn:aws:sns
:us-east-1:your-account
-id:TodoNotifications',
    Message=json.dumps({'default':
f'New todo item created: {todo_item}'}),
    MessageStructure='json'
)

return {
    'statusCode': 201,
    'body': json.dumps(todo_item)
}
```

Step 3: Deploy the Updated Application

Deploy the updated application using the Serverless Framework:

```bash
Copy code
serverless deploy
```

Step 4: Testing the SNS Integration

To test the SNS integration, create a new todo item using the create endpoint as described earlier. Once the item is created, you should receive a notification in the SNS topic.

To view the messages published to the SNS topic, you can create an SNS subscription. For example, you can subscribe an email endpoint to receive notifications:

1. In the SNS console, select the TodoNotifications topic.

117

2. Click on "Subscriptions" and then "Create subscription."

3. Choose "Email" as the protocol and enter your email address.

4. After creating the subscription, check your email and confirm the subscription.

Step 5: Additional Enhancements

To further enhance your event-driven architecture, consider integrating additional AWS services, such as:

- **Amazon SQS**: Use Amazon Simple Queue Service (SQS) for processing tasks asynchronously. Messages can be sent to SQS when todo items are created, allowing background processing without blocking the API.
- **AWS Step Functions**: Create complex workflows that orchestrate multiple Lambda functions and services. Use AWS Step Functions to manage state and coordinate event-driven processes.
- **Amazon Kinesis**: For real-time data processing, consider using Amazon Kinesis to collect and process streaming data. You can trigger Lambda functions based on Kinesis events for scenarios like real-time analytics.

Building a Real-World Example: Event-Driven Todo Application

To demonstrate the power of event-driven architectures in serverless applications, let's build a more comprehensive example. We will create an event-driven todo application that not only stores todo items but also triggers notifications and analytics when items are created or updated.

Overview of the Application

In this application, we will implement the following features:

1. Create todo items and store them in DynamoDB.

2. Send notifications via SNS when a todo item is created or updated.

3. Store analytics data (e.g., number of todos created) in another DynamoDB table.

Step 1: Create an Analytics DynamoDB Table

Create a new DynamoDB table named TodoAnalytics to store analytics data. You can do this using the AWS Management Console or the AWS CLI:

```bash
Copy code
aws dynamodb create-table \
    --table-name TodoAnalytics \
    --attribute-definitions \
        AttributeName=id,AttributeType=S \
    --key-schema \
        AttributeName=id,KeyType=HASH \
    --provisioned-throughput \
        ReadCapacityUnits=1,WriteCapacityUnits=1
```

Step 2: Modify the serverless.yml Configuration File

Update the serverless.yml file to include the new DynamoDB table and permissions for the analytics operations:

```yaml
Copy code
service: todo-lambda

provider:
  name: aws
  runtime: python3.8
  iamRoleStatements:
    - Effect: Allow
      Action:
```

```yaml
      - sns:Publish
      - dynamodb:PutItem
    Resource:
      - arn:aws:dynamodb:us-east-1
:your-account-id:table/Todos
      -
      arn:aws:dynamodb:us-east-1:your-account-id:table/TodoAnalytics

functions:
  create:
    handler: handler.create
    events:
      - http:
          path: todos
          method: post

  get_all:
    handler: handler.get_all
    events:
      - http:
          path: todos
          method: get

  update:
    handler: handler.update
    events:
      - http:
          path: todos/{id}
          method: put

  delete:
    handler: handler.delete
    events:
      - http:
          path: todos/{id}
          method: delete
```

Step 3: Update the Lambda Functions

Update the create and update functions in the handler.py file to store analytics data in the TodoAnalytics table:

```python
Copy code
analytics_table = dynamodb.Table('TodoAnalytics')

def create(event, context):
    body = json.loads(event['body'])
    todo_id = str(uuid.uuid4())
    todo_item = {
        'id': todo_id,
        'task': body['task'],
        'completed': False
    }

    table.put_item(Item=todo_item)

    # Publish a message to SNS
    sns.publish(
        TopicArn='arn:aws:sns
:us-east-1:your-account-id:TodoNotifications',
        Message=json.dumps({'default':
 f'New todo item created: {todo_item}'}),
        MessageStructure='json'
    )

    # Update analytics
    analytics_table.put_item(Item={'id':
'total_created', 'count': 1})

    return {
        'statusCode': 201,
        'body': json.dumps(todo_item)
    }

def update(event, context):
```

```
    todo_id = event['pathParameters']['id']
    body = json.loads(event['body'])
    completed = body.get('completed')

    table.update_item(
        Key={'id': todo_id},
        UpdateExpression='SET completed = :val',
        ExpressionAttributeValues=
{':val': completed}
    )

    # Publish a message to SNS
    sns.publish(
        TopicArn='arn:aws:sns
:us-east-1:your-account-id:TodoNotifications',
        Message=json.dumps({'default':
 f'Todo item updated: {todo_id},
 Completed: {completed}'}),
        MessageStructure='json'
    )

    return {
        'statusCode': 200,
        'body': json.dumps({'id': todo_id,
 'completed': completed})
    }
```

Step 4: Deploy the Updated Application

Deploy the updated application using the Serverless Framework:

```bash
Copy code
serverless deploy
```

Step 5: Testing the Enhanced Application

To test the enhanced application, create and update todo items as described in previous steps. Verify that notifications are sent via SNS and that analytics data is updated in the TodoAnalytics table.

Conclusion

In this chapter, we explored the principles of event-driven architectures and their application in serverless computing. We learned how to create event-driven workflows using AWS Lambda and various AWS services, such as DynamoDB and SNS.

By implementing event-driven architectures, you can build scalable, responsive, and decoupled applications that react to real-time events. In the next chapter, we will explore advanced techniques for optimizing serverless applications, including performance tuning, cost management, and architectural patterns for achieving high availability and resilience.

Chapter 10: Advanced Techniques for Optimizing Serverless Applications

As organizations increasingly adopt serverless architectures, optimizing these applications becomes paramount. Serverless computing provides inherent scalability and flexibility, but developers must consider performance tuning, cost management, and architectural patterns to achieve the best results. This chapter delves into advanced techniques for optimizing serverless applications, focusing on AWS Lambda and related services.

Understanding Optimization in Serverless Applications

What Does Optimization Mean?

Optimization in the context of serverless applications involves improving various aspects, including:

- **Performance**: Enhancing the speed and efficiency of application execution, reducing latency, and ensuring quick responses to user requests.
- **Cost Management**: Minimizing operational costs associated with serverless computing, including compute time, memory usage, and

external service calls.

- **Scalability**: Ensuring that applications can handle varying workloads without degradation in performance or user experience.
- **Reliability**: Building resilient applications that maintain functionality and availability, even in the face of failures or high traffic.

Why Optimization is Important

1. **User Experience**: Performance directly impacts user satisfaction. Slow response times can lead to frustration and abandonment of applications.
2. **Cost Efficiency**: Serverless architectures often charge based on usage. Optimizing performance and resource consumption can lead to significant cost savings.
3. **Resource Utilization**: Efficient use of cloud resources reduces waste and ensures that applications can scale seamlessly in response to demand.
4. **Operational Stability**: Optimization enhances the reliability and resilience of applications, ensuring they remain operational under various conditions.

Performance Tuning in Serverless Applications

Performance tuning focuses on optimizing the execution of serverless functions to ensure they respond quickly and efficiently to requests.

1. Reducing Cold Start Latency

Cold starts occur when AWS Lambda functions are invoked after a period of inactivity, leading to increased latency as the function is initialized. Here are techniques to mitigate cold start issues:

Use Provisioned Concurrency

Provisioned concurrency ensures that a specified number of instances of a Lambda function are pre-initialized and ready to respond to requests. This eliminates cold starts for those invocations, improving performance.

- **Configuration**: You can configure provisioned concurrency in the Serverless Framework by adding the following to your serverless.yml file:

```yaml
Copy code
functions:
  hello:
    handler: handler.hello
    provisionedConcurrency: 5
```

This setting maintains five warm instances of the function.

Optimize Deployment Package Size

Smaller deployment packages load faster. To reduce the size of your Lambda function, consider:

- **Removing Unused Dependencies**: Review and eliminate any unnecessary libraries or dependencies.
- **Using Layers**: AWS Lambda Layers allow you to package common dependencies separately, reducing the size of your function package.

Choose the Right Runtime

The choice of runtime can impact cold start times. For example, languages like Python and Node.js generally have faster cold starts than Java or .NET due to their lighter weight.

2. Efficient Memory and Timeout Settings

AWS Lambda allows you to configure the memory allocated to your functions, which directly affects CPU performance. Adjusting these settings can optimize execution speed.

Memory Configuration

Higher memory settings increase CPU allocation and can reduce execution time for compute-intensive tasks. Conduct performance testing to find the optimal memory allocation for your functions.

- **Configuration Example**:

```yaml
Copy code
functions:
  hello:
    handler: handler.hello
    memorySize: 512  # Increase memory allocation
```

Timeout Settings

Set appropriate timeout values for your functions. A longer timeout can be useful for functions performing complex operations, but excessive timeout settings may mask underlying performance issues.

- **Configuration Example**:

```yaml
Copy code
functions:
  hello:
    handler: handler.hello
    timeout: 30  # Set timeout to 30 seconds
```

3. Minimize External Calls

External service calls can introduce latency in your serverless applications. To optimize performance:

Batch Requests

When interacting with external services (e.g., databases, APIs), consider batching requests. This reduces the number of individual calls and can improve overall response times.

Use Caching

Implement caching strategies to reduce the need for repetitive calls to external services. AWS provides several caching solutions:

- **Amazon ElastiCache**: A managed Redis or Memcached service for caching data.
- **API Gateway Caching**: Cache responses from API Gateway to reduce latency for repeated requests.

4. Use Asynchronous Processing

For operations that do not require immediate responses, consider using asynchronous processing. AWS Lambda supports event-driven architectures that allow you to decouple processing tasks.

Amazon SQS and SNS Integration

Use Amazon Simple Queue Service (SQS) or Simple Notification Service (SNS) to handle background tasks asynchronously. For example, you can send messages to SQS after creating a todo item, triggering another Lambda function to process the message later.

5. Optimize Database Interactions

Efficient database interactions are critical for performance. Use the following techniques to optimize your database calls:

Connection Management

Establishing new database connections can be time-consuming. Utilize connection pooling or keep connections open to reduce latency in Lambda functions.

DynamoDB Best Practices

If using DynamoDB, consider the following best practices:

- **Use Batch Operations**: Leverage batch reads and writes to reduce the number of individual calls.
- **Choose Appropriate Read/Write Capacity**: Set appropriate provisioned capacity settings or enable on-demand mode to optimize costs.

Cost Management in Serverless Applications

Cost management is a crucial aspect of optimizing serverless applications. Since serverless architectures are billed based on usage, understanding and controlling costs can lead to significant savings.

1. Monitoring Usage and Costs

AWS provides several tools for monitoring costs associated with serverless applications:

AWS Cost Explorer

Use AWS Cost Explorer to visualize and analyze your AWS spending. You can filter costs by service, region, and tags to gain insights into where your money is going.

AWS Budgets

Set up AWS Budgets to receive alerts when your spending exceeds predefined thresholds. This proactive approach helps you manage costs and avoid unexpected charges.

2. Optimize Lambda Execution

Use the Right Memory Size

As mentioned earlier, the memory allocated to Lambda functions affects pricing. While higher memory settings can improve performance, it also increases costs. Conduct performance testing to find the right balance.

3. Optimize API Gateway Costs

API Gateway charges based on the number of requests and data transfer. To optimize costs:

Use Caching

Enable caching in API Gateway to reduce the number of requests to your Lambda functions. This can significantly decrease costs for frequently accessed data.

Set Appropriate Throttling Limits

Configure throttling limits for your API endpoints to prevent excessive requests from overwhelming your Lambda functions. This helps manage costs during traffic spikes.

4. Review and Optimize Third-Party Service Costs

If your serverless application interacts with third-party services (e.g., databases, external APIs), monitor and review the associated costs. Look for ways to optimize usage or switch to more cost-effective solutions.

Architectural Patterns for Serverless Applications

When designing serverless applications, it's essential to consider architectural patterns that enhance scalability, reliability, and maintainability.

1. Microservices Architecture

Microservices architecture promotes the development of small, independent services that communicate over well-defined APIs. In a serverless context, each microservice can be implemented as a separate AWS Lambda function, allowing for scalability and independent deployment.

2. Event-Driven Microservices

Combining event-driven architecture with microservices allows for efficient communication between services. Services can publish and subscribe to events, enabling them to react to changes in real-time. This approach promotes decoupling and scalability.

3. API Gateway as a Front Door

Using API Gateway as the entry point for your serverless application provides several benefits, including security, monitoring, and traffic management. API Gateway can route requests to the appropriate Lambda functions and handle authentication and authorization.

4. Step Functions for Orchestration

AWS Step Functions allow you to define workflows that coordinate multiple AWS services and Lambda functions. This is particularly useful for complex applications that require orchestration of multiple processes or tasks.

5. Handling Errors and Retries

Implement robust error handling and retry strategies in your serverless applications. Use AWS Lambda's built-in retry capabilities for asynchronous invocations, and consider using Dead Letter Queues (DLQ) for failed events.

Best Practices for Optimizing Serverless Applications

To ensure optimal performance, cost efficiency, and reliability in your serverless applications, consider the following best practices:

1. Regularly Review and Update Dependencies

Keep your application dependencies up to date to take advantage of performance improvements, security patches, and bug fixes.

2. Conduct Performance Testing

Regularly test the performance of your Lambda functions and APIs under different load conditions. Use tools like AWS X-Ray to trace requests and identify bottlenecks.

3. Use Infrastructure as Code (IaC)

Leverage Infrastructure as Code tools, such as AWS CloudFormation or the Serverless Framework, to manage your serverless resources consistently and version them alongside your code.

4. Monitor for Anomalies

Implement monitoring and alerting to detect unusual patterns or anomalies in application performance. This helps you respond proactively to potential issues.

5. Document Architectural Decisions

Maintain clear documentation of your serverless architecture, including design decisions and dependencies. This will aid future development and maintenance efforts.

6. Foster a Culture of Optimization

Encourage your team to prioritize optimization as part of the development process. Regularly review application performance and costs to identify areas for improvement.

Conclusion

In this chapter, we explored advanced techniques for optimizing serverless applications, focusing on performance tuning, cost management, and architectural patterns. By implementing best practices and leveraging the capabilities of AWS services, you can build efficient, scalable, and cost-effective serverless applications.

As serverless computing continues to evolve, staying informed about new features, best practices, and emerging patterns will be essential for maximizing the benefits of serverless architectures. In the next chapter, we will discuss real-world case studies and examples of successful serverless applications, highlighting their design choices, challenges faced, and lessons learned.

Chapter 11: Real-World Case Studies of Serverless Applications

s organizations transition to serverless architectures, numerous successful implementations showcase the benefits and flexibility of this model. This chapter explores real-world case studies of serverless applications built on AWS, detailing their design choices, the challenges faced during development, and the lessons learned. By examining these examples, we can glean valuable insights into best practices for designing and deploying serverless applications.

Case Study 1: Netflix

Overview

Netflix, the leading streaming service provider, leverages serverless computing to enhance its data processing capabilities. With millions of users worldwide, Netflix generates vast amounts of data that require efficient processing and analysis. By adopting serverless architectures, Netflix has improved its ability to handle data at scale while optimizing costs.

Architecture and Design Choices

Netflix's serverless architecture utilizes AWS Lambda for processing real-time data streams and events generated by user interactions. Key components of their architecture include:

- **AWS Lambda**: Handles event-driven data processing for tasks such as logging user activities, analyzing viewing patterns, and managing content recommendations.
- **Amazon Kinesis**: Serves as the event source for real-time data streaming. It collects user activity data, which triggers Lambda functions for processing.
- **Amazon S3**: Stores large volumes of processed data, enabling Netflix to maintain a data lake for analytics.
- **Amazon DynamoDB**: Acts as a fast NoSQL database for storing user preferences and recommendation data.

Challenges Faced

1. **Cold Start Latency**: With a large number of Lambda functions handling various data processing tasks, Netflix experienced latency issues due to cold starts.
2. **Monitoring and Debugging**: As the architecture grew more complex, monitoring and debugging serverless functions became challenging. The need for effective observability tools was crucial.
3. **Cost Management**: With increasing usage and data volumes, managing costs while maintaining performance was a significant concern.

Lessons Learned

- **Utilize Provisioned Concurrency**: By implementing provisioned concurrency for critical functions, Netflix was able to reduce cold start latency significantly, ensuring faster response times.

- **Invest in Monitoring Tools**: Implementing robust monitoring and logging solutions (such as AWS CloudWatch and custom dashboards) allowed Netflix to gain visibility into function performance, identify bottlenecks, and streamline debugging efforts.
- **Optimize Resource Usage**: Regularly reviewing and optimizing the architecture based on usage patterns helped Netflix manage costs while maintaining performance.

Case Study 2: Coca-Cola

Overview

Coca-Cola employs serverless architectures to enhance its digital marketing campaigns and improve customer engagement. By leveraging AWS Lambda and other serverless services, Coca-Cola aims to streamline operations and deliver personalized experiences to consumers.

Architecture and Design Choices

Coca-Cola's serverless architecture is designed to handle various aspects of its marketing efforts:

- **AWS Lambda**: Processes data from multiple sources, including social media interactions, user surveys, and mobile applications.
- **Amazon API Gateway**: Serves as the entry point for mobile and web applications, allowing seamless communication between front-end applications and backend services.
- **Amazon DynamoDB**: Stores user interaction data and preferences, facilitating targeted marketing efforts.
- **Amazon S3**: Houses multimedia assets, including images and videos, used in marketing campaigns.

Challenges Faced

1. **Data Integration**: With multiple data sources feeding into the system, integrating and processing this data in real time was a complex challenge.
2. **Scalability**: During major marketing campaigns, user engagement spikes significantly, putting pressure on the serverless architecture to scale effectively.
3. **Personalization**: Ensuring that marketing campaigns are personalized and relevant to users based on their interactions and preferences required sophisticated data processing capabilities.

Lessons Learned

- **Use Event-Driven Architecture**: Implementing an event-driven architecture allowed Coca-Cola to react to user interactions in real time, delivering timely and relevant content.
- **Implement Efficient Caching Strategies**: To handle spikes in traffic during campaigns, Coca-Cola utilized caching mechanisms (such as Amazon ElastiCache) to reduce the load on Lambda functions and improve response times.
- **Focus on User Experience**: By analyzing user data and behavior patterns, Coca-Cola was able to enhance the personalization of its marketing campaigns, leading to increased customer engagement.

Case Study 3: iRobot

Overview

iRobot, the creator of the popular Roomba vacuum cleaning robot, utilizes serverless architectures to enhance its connected home products. By leveraging AWS Lambda, iRobot aims to improve the performance of its cloud services and provide a seamless user experience.

Architecture and Design Choices

iRobot's architecture incorporates several AWS services to support its cloud-based functionalities:

- **AWS Lambda**: Handles event processing for various user interactions, including app commands and sensor data from Roomba devices.
- **Amazon API Gateway**: Provides a RESTful API for mobile applications, allowing users to control their robots and access data remotely.
- **Amazon DynamoDB**: Stores user preferences, schedules, and historical data on cleaning tasks.
- **Amazon SNS**: Sends notifications to users regarding device status and updates.

Challenges Faced

1. **Device Communication**: Managing real-time communication between the cloud and devices required efficient handling of events and state management.
2. **Latency Concerns**: Users expect instant responses when controlling their devices, making latency a critical factor.
3. **Scaling Issues**: As iRobot introduced new features and devices, ensuring the infrastructure could scale appropriately was essential.

Lessons Learned

- **Optimize API Gateway Settings**: By fine-tuning API Gateway settings (e.g., throttling and caching), iRobot reduced response times and improved user experience during peak usage.
- **Implement Effective Data Management**: Using DynamoDB's capabilities, iRobot effectively managed user preferences and historical data, allowing for personalized user experiences.
- **Utilize AWS IoT**: Integrating AWS IoT Core for device communication

improved the reliability and scalability of interactions between the cloud and devices.

Case Study 4: Unilever

Overview

Unilever, a global consumer goods company, leverages serverless architectures to enhance its product development processes and marketing strategies. By utilizing AWS Lambda, Unilever aims to improve data analytics and customer engagement.

Architecture and Design Choices

Unilever's architecture involves multiple AWS services to support its business operations:

- **AWS Lambda**: Processes data from various sources, including market research, customer feedback, and social media analytics.
- **Amazon Kinesis**: Collects and processes streaming data in real time, enabling Unilever to analyze trends and consumer preferences.
- **Amazon S3**: Stores vast amounts of data related to product performance and marketing efforts.
- **Amazon QuickSight**: Provides data visualization and reporting capabilities to stakeholders.

Challenges Faced

1. **Data Volume**: Managing and processing large volumes of data from multiple sources posed significant challenges.
2. **Real-Time Insights**: Delivering real-time insights for decision-making required efficient data processing and analytics capabilities.
3. **Integration of Multiple Data Sources**: Combining data from various

internal and external sources to generate actionable insights was complex.

Lessons Learned

- **Leverage Real-Time Data Processing**: By utilizing Amazon Kinesis for real-time data processing, Unilever was able to gain immediate insights into market trends and consumer behavior.
- **Implement Data Governance Practices**: Establishing data governance practices ensured data quality and compliance, allowing Unilever to trust its analytics.
- **Optimize Visualization Tools**: Integrating AWS QuickSight with Lambda functions enabled Unilever to create dynamic dashboards for stakeholders, facilitating data-driven decision-making.

Case Study 5: Slack

Overview

Slack, the popular collaboration and messaging platform, utilizes serverless architectures to enhance its user experience and scalability. By leveraging AWS Lambda, Slack can efficiently handle user interactions and backend processes.

Architecture and Design Choices

Slack's architecture is designed to support millions of active users and their interactions:

- **AWS Lambda**: Processes incoming messages, notifications, and integrations with external services.
- **Amazon DynamoDB**: Stores user preferences, message histories, and channel data.

- **Amazon SQS**: Manages asynchronous processing of background tasks and notifications.

Challenges Faced

1. **Scalability**: Handling rapid user growth and peak usage times posed challenges for the underlying infrastructure.
2. **Latency**: Users expect near-instantaneous message delivery and interaction responsiveness.
3. **Integration with Third-Party Services**: Integrating with various third-party applications and services required efficient management of events and workflows.

Lessons Learned

- **Implement Event-Driven Workflows**: By leveraging an event-driven architecture, Slack effectively managed user interactions and ensured real-time processing of messages.
- **Optimize Database Performance**: Regularly monitoring and optimizing DynamoDB performance allowed Slack to handle increased loads and reduce latency.
- **Leverage Asynchronous Processing**: Utilizing SQS for background tasks and notifications improved the overall responsiveness of the application, ensuring that user interactions remained fluid.

Key Takeaways from Case Studies

1. **Embrace Event-Driven Architectures**: Event-driven architectures enable serverless applications to react to real-time events, enhancing scalability and responsiveness.
2. **Leverage AWS Services**: Integrating various AWS services (e.g., Lambda, DynamoDB, SNS, SQS) provides powerful capabilities for building resilient and efficient serverless applications.

3. **Focus on Monitoring and Optimization**: Regular monitoring, testing, and optimization are crucial for maintaining performance and managing costs in serverless architectures.

4. **Prioritize User Experience**: Enhancing user experience through responsive designs, low latency, and personalized interactions is essential for the success of serverless applications.

5. **Implement Robust Security Practices**: Ensuring security through authentication, authorization, and data protection is vital in serverless applications, particularly when handling sensitive user data.

Conclusion

This chapter explored real-world case studies of organizations successfully implementing serverless architectures. By examining their design choices, challenges, and lessons learned, we can glean valuable insights for building and optimizing serverless applications.

As serverless computing continues to evolve, organizations can leverage these best practices and experiences to create efficient, scalable, and user-centric applications. In the next chapter, we will explore the future of serverless computing, emerging trends, and how organizations can prepare for the next generation of cloud-native applications.

Chapter 12: The Future of Serverless Computing

As organizations increasingly adopt cloud technologies, serverless computing has emerged as a transformative model that reshapes how applications are developed, deployed, and managed. The convenience of building applications without the burden of managing infrastructure has led to widespread adoption across various industries. This chapter explores the future of serverless computing, highlighting emerging trends, challenges, and opportunities for developers and organizations looking to leverage this powerful paradigm.

Understanding the Evolution of Serverless Computing

A Brief History of Serverless Computing

Serverless computing is not a new concept; its roots can be traced back to the early 2000s with the introduction of cloud services. However, the term "serverless" gained popularity with the launch of AWS Lambda in 2014. This marked a significant shift in how developers approached application development, allowing them to focus on writing code without worrying about the underlying infrastructure.

Key Milestones in Serverless Evolution

1. **Introduction of Function-as-a-Service (FaaS)**: AWS Lambda pioneered the FaaS model, enabling developers to deploy individual functions that respond to events without the need for provisioning or managing servers.
2. **Rise of Managed Services**: Alongside FaaS, cloud providers began offering various managed services (e.g., databases, storage, messaging) that seamlessly integrate with serverless architectures.
3. **Adoption of Microservices Architecture**: The combination of serverless computing and microservices architecture allowed organizations to build applications as a collection of loosely coupled services, enhancing scalability and maintainability.
4. **Expansion Beyond AWS**: Other cloud providers, such as Microsoft Azure and Google Cloud Platform, introduced their serverless offerings, increasing competition and innovation in the space.
5. **Emergence of Serverless Frameworks**: Open-source frameworks like the Serverless Framework, AWS SAM, and Terraform simplified the development and deployment of serverless applications, promoting best practices and standardization.

Emerging Trends in Serverless Computing

As the serverless landscape continues to evolve, several trends are shaping its future. Understanding these trends will help organizations stay ahead of the curve and fully leverage the benefits of serverless computing.

1. Increased Adoption of Multi-Cloud Strategies

Organizations are increasingly adopting multi-cloud strategies to avoid vendor lock-in, enhance resilience, and optimize costs. This trend allows organizations to choose the best services from multiple cloud providers based on specific requirements.

Benefits of Multi-Cloud Strategies

- **Flexibility**: Organizations can select the most suitable services from different providers, enabling them to build more effective solutions.
- **Resilience**: Distributing workloads across multiple cloud providers enhances availability and reduces the risk of downtime due to provider-specific issues.
- **Cost Optimization**: Organizations can take advantage of competitive pricing and features offered by different cloud providers.

2. Serverless Containerization

Containerization and serverless computing are converging as organizations look to combine the benefits of both technologies. While serverless computing abstracts infrastructure management, containerization provides portability and consistency across environments.

Benefits of Serverless Containers

- **Portability**: Containers can run consistently across different environments, making it easier to move applications between development, testing, and production.
- **Fine-Grained Control**: Using containers allows developers to package their applications with all dependencies, ensuring that they run as intended.
- **Optimized Resource Usage**: Serverless containers enable organizations to optimize resource usage by dynamically scaling containers based on demand.

3. Enhanced Security Measures

As serverless applications become more prevalent, the need for robust security measures will continue to grow. Organizations must address potential vulnerabilities unique to serverless architectures, such as event injection and API security.

Trends in Serverless Security

- **Security Automation**: The adoption of security automation tools will streamline the identification and remediation of vulnerabilities in serverless applications.
- **API Security**: With the increased reliance on APIs in serverless architectures, organizations will prioritize API security measures, including authentication, authorization, and rate limiting.
- **Compliance and Governance**: Organizations will focus on ensuring compliance with industry regulations (e.g., GDPR, HIPAA) by implementing governance frameworks and security best practices.

4. Advancements in Observability and Monitoring

As serverless applications grow in complexity, the demand for enhanced observability and monitoring solutions will increase. Organizations need to gain deeper insights into application performance, user behavior, and system health.

Trends in Observability

- **Real-Time Analytics**: The rise of real-time analytics tools will enable organizations to monitor serverless applications continuously, identifying and addressing issues proactively.
- **Distributed Tracing**: Implementing distributed tracing will provide visibility into the flow of requests across multiple services, making it easier to diagnose performance bottlenecks and errors.
- **Integration with AI and ML**: Leveraging artificial intelligence and machine learning for monitoring will allow organizations to predict performance issues and optimize resource allocation.

5. Serverless Beyond Traditional Use Cases

While serverless computing has primarily been associated with web applications and microservices, its potential extends to various use cases, including:

- **Machine Learning**: Serverless architectures can be used to deploy and scale machine learning models, enabling organizations to process data and generate predictions without managing infrastructure.
- **Internet of Things (IoT)**: Serverless computing can facilitate real-time processing of IoT data streams, enabling organizations to analyze and respond to events generated by connected devices.
- **Data Processing and ETL**: Organizations can leverage serverless functions for data processing and extraction, transformation, and loading (ETL) tasks, enhancing the efficiency of data workflows.

Challenges and Considerations for Serverless Computing

While the future of serverless computing is promising, organizations must address several challenges and considerations to maximize the benefits of this architecture.

1. Vendor Lock-In

One of the significant challenges of serverless computing is the potential for vendor lock-in. Organizations relying heavily on a single cloud provider may face challenges when attempting to migrate to another platform or integrate with third-party services.

Mitigating Vendor Lock-In

- **Adopt Open Standards**: Leverage open standards and technologies that can be easily transferred between cloud providers.
- **Implement Multi-Cloud Strategies**: Adopt a multi-cloud approach to diversify dependencies and reduce reliance on a single vendor.

- **Use Abstraction Layers**: Consider using abstraction layers or frameworks that facilitate deployment across multiple cloud providers.

2. Cold Start Issues

Cold starts, where serverless functions experience latency during initialization, can impact user experience, especially in latency-sensitive applications. While techniques like provisioned concurrency can help, they may also increase costs.

Strategies to Mitigate Cold Starts

- **Use Provisioned Concurrency**: Configure provisioned concurrency for critical functions to reduce cold start latency.
- **Optimize Function Size**: Reduce the size of deployment packages to improve initialization time.
- **Choose Faster Runtimes**: Select runtimes known for faster cold start performance, such as Node.js or Python.

3. Monitoring Complexity

As serverless applications grow in complexity, monitoring and debugging can become challenging. Organizations must ensure they have adequate observability into the entire application stack.

Implementing Effective Monitoring

- **Centralize Logs and Metrics**: Use centralized logging and monitoring tools to aggregate logs and metrics from various services.
- **Adopt Distributed Tracing**: Implement distributed tracing solutions to gain insights into request flows and identify performance bottlenecks.
- **Regularly Review Metrics**: Establish a routine for reviewing key metrics and logs to identify trends and anomalies proactively.

4. Testing and Debugging Challenges

Testing and debugging serverless applications can be more complicated due to their distributed nature. Traditional testing methodologies may not suffice.

Strategies for Effective Testing

- **Use Local Development Tools**: Utilize local development tools and emulators (e.g., SAM CLI, LocalStack) to simulate AWS services for testing.
- **Implement Automated Testing**: Incorporate unit tests, integration tests, and end-to-end tests into the CI/CD pipeline to ensure the reliability of serverless functions.
- **Conduct Load Testing**: Perform load testing to simulate real-world usage and identify potential bottlenecks.

Preparing for the Future of Serverless Computing

As the serverless landscape continues to evolve, organizations should proactively prepare for the future by adopting best practices and staying informed about emerging trends.

1. Embrace a Serverless Culture

Fostering a serverless culture within the organization encourages innovation and agility. This includes providing training and resources for developers to understand serverless concepts and tools.

2. Invest in Skill Development

Continuous learning and upskilling are essential for staying competitive in the serverless landscape. Encourage developers to pursue certifications, attend workshops, and participate in online courses related to serverless technologies.

3. Collaborate Across Teams

Encouraging collaboration between development, operations, and security teams can lead to better outcomes when implementing serverless architectures. Cross-functional teams can ensure that security, performance, and operational concerns are addressed during development.

4. Monitor Industry Trends

Stay informed about industry trends and advancements in serverless computing. Attend conferences, webinars, and community events to learn from experts and peers.

5. Experiment and Innovate

Encourage teams to experiment with new serverless tools, architectures, and patterns. Innovation drives progress, and allowing teams to explore new ideas can lead to valuable insights and improvements.

Conclusion

In this chapter, we explored the future of serverless computing, examining emerging trends, challenges, and considerations for organizations looking to leverage this powerful paradigm. As serverless architectures continue to evolve, they will play a pivotal role in shaping the future of application development and deployment.

By understanding the implications of these trends and adopting best practices, organizations can position themselves for success in the rapidly changing landscape of cloud-native applications. In the final chapter, we will summarize the key takeaways from this book and provide guidance for embarking on your serverless journey.

Chapter 13: The Serverless Journey – Key Takeaways and Future Directions

I n the rapidly evolving landscape of cloud computing, serverless architecture has emerged as a transformative approach to application development and deployment. This chapter aims to summarize the key takeaways from the preceding chapters, emphasizing the critical aspects of serverless computing and offering insights into the future directions of this technology. As organizations embark on their serverless journeys, understanding these elements will be essential for success in building scalable, cost-effective, and resilient applications.

Key Takeaways from the Book

1. Understanding Serverless Architecture

Serverless architecture represents a paradigm shift in how applications are built and managed. It allows developers to focus on writing code without the overhead of infrastructure management. Key aspects of serverless architecture include:

- **Event-Driven Computing**: Serverless functions are invoked in response to events, enabling real-time processing and responsiveness.

- **Function as a Service (FaaS)**: Serverless computing is often implemented through FaaS offerings, such as AWS Lambda, where individual functions perform specific tasks in an application.
- **Managed Services**: Serverless architectures rely on various managed services (e.g., databases, message queues, storage) that integrate seamlessly with serverless functions.

2. Benefits of Serverless Computing

Organizations adopting serverless architectures can enjoy several benefits, including:

- **Scalability**: Serverless applications can automatically scale based on demand, allowing organizations to handle varying workloads without manual intervention.
- **Cost Efficiency**: With a pay-as-you-go pricing model, serverless computing reduces costs by charging only for the resources consumed during function execution.
- **Faster Time to Market**: By abstracting infrastructure management, serverless architecture enables developers to focus on building features, leading to quicker deployment cycles.
- **Reduced Operational Overhead**: Serverless computing minimizes the need for system administration and maintenance, allowing teams to concentrate on development and innovation.

3. Designing Serverless Applications

Designing effective serverless applications requires careful consideration of architecture, event sources, and integration with managed services. Key design principles include:

- **Microservices Architecture**: Adopting a microservices approach allows for the development of independent services that can be deployed and scaled independently.

- **Event-Driven Workflows**: Implementing event-driven architectures enables applications to respond dynamically to user interactions and system events.
- **API Gateway as the Front Door**: Using API Gateway provides a secure and manageable entry point for serverless applications, allowing for routing and monitoring of API requests.

4. Performance Optimization Techniques

Optimizing the performance of serverless applications is crucial for ensuring responsiveness and user satisfaction. Techniques for performance tuning include:

- **Reducing Cold Start Latency**: Implementing strategies such as provisioned concurrency, optimizing function sizes, and selecting appropriate runtimes can minimize cold start latency.
- **Efficient Memory and Timeout Settings**: Adjusting memory allocations and timeout settings based on application requirements can enhance execution speed and reduce costs.
- **Minimizing External Calls**: Using batching, caching, and asynchronous processing can optimize interactions with external services, reducing latency and improving overall performance.

5. Cost Management Strategies

Managing costs effectively is essential for organizations utilizing serverless architectures. Key strategies include:

- **Monitoring Usage and Costs**: Utilizing tools like AWS Cost Explorer and AWS Budgets helps organizations track spending and identify cost-saving opportunities.
- **Optimizing Lambda Execution**: Regularly reviewing and adjusting

memory settings and optimizing API Gateway configurations can help control costs while maintaining performance.

- **Reviewing Third-Party Service Costs**: Monitoring and optimizing interactions with third-party services can prevent unexpected expenses and ensure efficient resource usage.

6. Security Considerations in Serverless Applications

Security is a critical concern for serverless applications, and organizations must implement robust security measures to protect data and resources. Key considerations include:

- **Authentication and Authorization**: Implementing proper authentication and authorization mechanisms, such as AWS IAM and Amazon Cognito, is essential for controlling access to serverless functions and APIs.
- **Data Protection**: Encrypting sensitive data in transit and at rest ensures that information remains secure and compliant with regulations.
- **Regular Security Audits**: Conducting regular security audits and reviews helps organizations identify vulnerabilities and improve their security posture.

7. Monitoring and Observability

Effective monitoring and observability are vital for maintaining the health and performance of serverless applications. Organizations should focus on:

- **Using CloudWatch for Metrics and Logs**: AWS CloudWatch provides metrics and logging capabilities that enable organizations to monitor serverless functions and troubleshoot issues effectively.
- **Implementing Distributed Tracing**: Utilizing tools like AWS X-Ray allows for visibility into request flows and performance bottlenecks across distributed components.

- **Regularly Reviewing Metrics**: Establishing a routine for reviewing key metrics helps organizations identify trends and proactively address potential issues.

8. The Importance of CI/CD in Serverless Development

Implementing Continuous Integration and Continuous Deployment (CI/CD) practices is essential for streamlining the development process of serverless applications. Key aspects include:

- **Automating Testing and Deployment**: Integrating automated testing and deployment into the development workflow ensures that code changes are validated before reaching production.
- **Utilizing Tools for CI/CD**: Leveraging tools like AWS CodePipeline and GitHub Actions can simplify the CI/CD process and enhance collaboration among teams.
- **Fostering a Culture of Optimization**: Encouraging teams to prioritize optimization as part of the development process can lead to improved performance and reliability.

9. Future Trends and Directions

The future of serverless computing is characterized by emerging trends and technologies that will shape its evolution. Organizations should stay informed about:

- **Multi-Cloud Strategies**: Adopting multi-cloud approaches can help organizations diversify dependencies and avoid vendor lock-in.
- **Serverless Containerization**: Combining serverless computing with containerization offers flexibility and portability for application deployment.
- **Enhanced Security Measures**: As serverless architectures gain popularity, investing in robust security practices will be crucial for protecting

sensitive data and maintaining compliance.

- **Advancements in Observability**: Continuous improvements in monitoring and observability tools will enable organizations to gain deeper insights into application performance.
- **Broader Use Cases**: Expanding the use of serverless computing to various domains, such as machine learning, IoT, and data processing, will unlock new opportunities for innovation.

Preparing for Your Serverless Journey

Embarking on a serverless journey requires careful planning and consideration. Organizations should follow these steps to prepare for successful implementation:

1. Assess Your Use Cases

Evaluate your application needs and determine whether serverless architecture is suitable for your use cases. Consider factors such as scalability, cost, and development timelines.

2. Choose the Right Tools and Frameworks

Select the appropriate tools and frameworks that align with your development processes. Options such as the Serverless Framework, AWS SAM, and Terraform can streamline deployment and management.

3. Foster a Serverless Mindset

Encourage a culture of innovation and experimentation within your organization. Foster collaboration between development, operations, and security teams to ensure the successful adoption of serverless practices.

4. Start Small and Iterate

Begin with small projects or proof-of-concept implementations to gain experience with serverless technologies. Use iterative development processes to refine your approach and learn from each implementation.

5. Invest in Training and Skill Development

Provide training opportunities for your development teams to enhance their understanding of serverless concepts and best practices. Encourage certification programs and knowledge-sharing sessions to build expertise.

6. Monitor and Adapt

Once your serverless applications are deployed, continuously monitor their performance and user feedback. Be prepared to adapt and iterate based on insights gained from usage patterns and evolving requirements.

Conclusion

As we conclude this journey through serverless computing, it's evident that serverless architectures represent a significant shift in how applications are built and managed. By embracing the principles of serverless computing, organizations can achieve enhanced scalability, cost efficiency, and flexibility.

This book has provided valuable insights into the key concepts, design patterns, and best practices for leveraging serverless technologies. As the landscape continues to evolve, staying informed about emerging trends and continuously optimizing your serverless applications will be essential for success.

The future of serverless computing is bright, and the opportunities it presents are vast. By harnessing the power of serverless architectures, organizations can innovate faster, respond to changing market demands, and deliver exceptional user experiences in the digital age.

Chapter 14: Building a Complete Full-Stack Application with Serverless Architecture

I n this chapter, we will delve into building a complete full-stack application using serverless architecture. This practical guide will help you understand the concepts, design patterns, and implementation details necessary to create a robust and scalable application. Our focus will be on using AWS services such as AWS Lambda, API Gateway, DynamoDB, and S3, combined with a front-end framework like React or Angular.

Project Overview: Todo List Application

We will build a simple Todo List application that allows users to create, read, update, and delete todo items. This application will illustrate how to leverage serverless architecture for both the front-end and back-end components.

Features of the Todo List Application

1. **User Authentication**: Users can register and log in to manage their todo items.
2. **CRUD Operations**: Users can create, read, update, and delete todo items.

3. **Persistent Data Storage**: Todo items will be stored in a DynamoDB table.

4. **Serverless API**: The backend will be built using AWS Lambda and API Gateway to expose a RESTful API.

5. **Responsive Front-End**: A user-friendly front-end built with React (or Angular) to interact with the backend.

Architecture Diagram

Before diving into the implementation, let's visualize the architecture of our Todo List application:

```scss
Copy code
User Interface (React/Angular)
        |
        | HTTP Requests (API Gateway)
        |
    API Gateway
        |
        | Trigger
        |
    AWS Lambda Functions
        |
        | Access
        |
    DynamoDB (Todo Items)
```

Step 1: Setting Up Your AWS Environment

Creating an AWS Account

If you don't already have an AWS account, you can create one at AWS Sign Up. AWS offers a free tier that allows you to experiment with various services without incurring costs.

Installing the AWS CLI

To manage your AWS resources from the command line, install the AWS Command Line Interface (CLI):

- **Installation**: Follow the instructions for your operating system on the AWS CLI Installation Guide.

Configuring the AWS CLI

After installation, configure the AWS CLI with your credentials:

```bash
Copy code
aws configure
```

You will be prompted to enter your AWS Access Key ID, Secret Access Key, region, and output format. These can be obtained from the IAM console in your AWS account.

Step 2: Setting Up the Backend with AWS Lambda and API Gateway

Creating the DynamoDB Table

We will use DynamoDB to store our todo items. Let's create a table named Todos.

Using the AWS Management Console

1. Log in to your AWS account and navigate to the DynamoDB service.
2. Click on "Create table."
3. Enter the following details:

- **Table name**: Todos
- **Partition key**: id (String)

1. Click on "Create."

Using the AWS CLI

Alternatively, you can create the DynamoDB table using the CLI:

```bash
Copy code
aws dynamodb create-table \
    --table-name Todos \
    --attribute-definitions \
        AttributeName=id,AttributeType=S \
    --key-schema \
        AttributeName=id,KeyType=HASH \
    --provisioned-throughput \
        ReadCapacityUnits=5,WriteCapacityUnits=5
```

Creating Lambda Functions

Next, we will create Lambda functions to handle the CRUD operations for our Todo List application.

1. **Create a directory for your project**:

```bash
Copy code
mkdir todo-serverless-app
cd todo-serverless-app
```

1. **Create a file named handler.py** for your Lambda functions:

```bash
Copy code
touch handler.py
```

1. **Implement the Lambda functions** in handler.py:

```python
Copy code
import json
import boto3
import uuid

dynamodb = boto3.resource('dynamodb')
table = dynamodb.Table('Todos')

def create(event, context):
    body = json.loads(event['body'])
    todo_id = str(uuid.uuid4())
    todo_item = {
        'id': todo_id,
        'task': body['task'],
        'completed': False
    }

    table.put_item(Item=todo_item)

    return {
        'statusCode': 201,
        'body': json.dumps(todo_item)
    }

def get_all(event, context):
    response = table.scan()
    todos = response.get('Items', [])
```

```python
    return {
        'statusCode': 200,
        'body': json.dumps(todos)
    }


def update(event, context):
    todo_id = event['pathParameters']['id']
    body = json.loads(event['body'])
    completed = body.get('completed')

    table.update_item(
        Key={'id': todo_id},
        UpdateExpression='SET completed = :val',
        ExpressionAttributeValues={':val': completed}
    )

    return {
        'statusCode': 200,
        'body': json.dumps({'id': todo_id, 'completed':
        completed})
    }

def delete(event, context):
    todo_id = event['pathParameters']['id']

    table.delete_item(Key={'id': todo_id})

    return {
        'statusCode': 204
    }
```

Setting Up API Gateway

To expose our Lambda functions as a RESTful API, we will use AWS API Gateway.

1. **Create a serverless.yml file** in your project directory to define the API Gateway and Lambda functions:

```yaml
yaml
Copy code
service: todo-serverless-app

provider:
  name: aws
  runtime: python3.8

functions:
  create:
    handler: handler.create
    events:
      - http:
          path: todos
          method: post

  get_all:
    handler: handler.get_all
    events:
      - http:
          path: todos
          method: get

  update:
    handler: handler.update
    events:
      - http:
          path: todos/{id}
          method: put

  delete:
    handler: handler.delete
    events:
      - http:
          path: todos/{id}
          method: delete
```

Deploying the Serverless Application

To deploy your serverless application, ensure you have the Serverless Framework installed. If you haven't done so, install it via npm:

```bash
Copy code
npm install -g serverless
```

Then deploy your application:

```bash
Copy code
serverless deploy
```

After the deployment, you will receive URLs for your API endpoints.

Step 3: Building the Frontend with React

Now that we have set up the backend, let's create a frontend application using React. This frontend will communicate with our serverless API to manage todo items.

Setting Up the React Application

1. **Create a new React application** using Create React App:

```bash
Copy code
npx create-react-app todo-frontend
cd todo-frontend
```

1. **Install Axios for HTTP Requests**:

```bash
Copy code
npm install axios
```

Implementing the Todo List Component

Now, we will create a component to manage our todo list.

1. **Create a new file named TodoList.js in the src directory**:

```bash
Copy code
touch src/TodoList.js
```

1. **Implement the Todo List component**:

```javascript
Copy code
import React, { useEffect, useState } from 'react';
import axios from 'axios';

const API_URL =
'https://<api-id>.execute-api.us-east-1.amazonaws.com/dev/todos';

const TodoList = () => {
    const [todos, setTodos] = useState([]);
    const [task, setTask] = useState('');
```

```
const fetchTodos = async () => {
    const response = await axios.get(API_URL);
    setTodos(response.data);
};

const addTodo = async () => {
    if (task) {
        await axios.post(API_URL, { task });
        setTask('');
        fetchTodos();
    }
};

const deleteTodo = async (id) => {
    await axios.delete(`${API_URL}/${id}`);
    fetchTodos();
};

const toggleComplete = async (todo) => {
    await axios.put(`${API_URL}/${todo.id}`, {
        completed: !todo.completed,
    });
    fetchTodos();
};

useEffect(() => {
    fetchTodos();
}, []);

return (
    <div>
        <h1>Todo List</h1>
        <input
            type="text"
            value={task}
            onChange={(e) => setTask(e.target.value)}
            placeholder="Add a new task"
        />
        <button onClick={addTodo}>Add Todo</button>
```

```
        <ul>
            {todos.map((todo) => (
                <li key={todo.id}>
                    <span
                        style={{ textDecoration:
                        todo.completed ? 'line-through' :
                        'none' }}
                        onClick={() => toggleComplete(todo)}
                    >
                        {todo.task}
                    </span>
                    <button onClick={() =>
                    deleteTodo(todo.id)}>Delete</button>
                </li>
            ))}
        </ul>
    </div>
  );
};

export default TodoList;
```

Updating the Main App Component

Now, update the App.js file to include the TodoList component:

```javascript
Copy code
import React from 'react';
import TodoList from './TodoList';

function App() {
    return (
        <div className="App">
            <TodoList />
        </div>
    );
```

```
}

export default App;
```

Running the React Application

1. **Start the development server**:

```bash
Copy code
npm start
```

1. **Access the application** at http://localhost:3000 and test the functionality of your Todo List application.

Step 4: Implementing User Authentication

To enhance our Todo List application, we'll implement user authentication using Amazon Cognito. This will allow users to register and log in to manage their todo items securely.

Setting Up Amazon Cognito

1. **Create a User Pool**:

- Navigate to the Amazon Cognito service in the AWS Management Console.
- Click on "Create a user pool" and configure it according to your requirements.
- Make note of the User Pool ID and App Client ID, as you will need them

for your application.

1. **Set Up User Pool Client**:

- In the User Pool settings, create an App Client without generating a client secret.
- Configure the App Client settings, including enabling authentication flows.

Updating the Frontend for Authentication

1. **Install Amazon Cognito Identity SDK**:

```bash
Copy code
npm install amazon-cognito-identity-js
```

1. **Create a new file named Auth.js in the src directory** to handle authentication logic:

```javascript
Copy code
import { CognitoUserPool, CognitoUser, AuthenticationDetails }
from 'amazon-cognito-identity-js';

const poolData = {
    UserPoolId: 'your-user-pool-id',
    ClientId: 'your-app-client-id',
};

const userPool = new CognitoUserPool(poolData);
```

```
export const registerUser = (username, password) => {
    return new Promise((resolve, reject) => {
        userPool.signUp(username, password, [], null, (err, data)
        => {
            if (err) {
                reject(err);
            } else {
                resolve(data);
            }
        });
    });
};


export const loginUser = (username, password) => {
    return new Promise((resolve, reject) => {
        const authenticationDetails = new AuthenticationDetails({
            Username: username,
            Password: password,
        });

        const user = new CognitoUser({ Username: username, Pool:
        userPool });

        user.authenticateUser(authenticationDetails, {
            onSuccess: (result) => {
                resolve(result);
            },
            onFailure: (err) => {
                reject(err);
            },
        });
    });
};
```

Creating Authentication Components

1. **Create a new file named AuthForm.js in the src directory** for user registration and login:

```javascript
Copy code
import React, { useState } from 'react';
import { registerUser, loginUser } from './Auth';

const AuthForm = ({ onAuth }) => {
    const [username, setUsername] = useState('');
    const [password, setPassword] = useState('');
    const [isRegistering, setIsRegistering] = useState(true);

    const handleSubmit = async (e) => {
        e.preventDefault();
        try {
            if (isRegistering) {
                await registerUser(username, password);
                alert('User registered successfully!');
            } else {
                const result = await loginUser(username,
                password);
                alert(`Logged in! Token:
                ${result.getAccessToken().getJwtToken()}`);
                onAuth(result.getAccessToken().getJwtToken());
            }
            setUsername('');
            setPassword('');
        } catch (error) {
            alert(error.message);
        }
    };

    return (
        <form onSubmit={handleSubmit}>
            <h2>{isRegistering ? 'Register' : 'Login'}</h2>
```

```
        <input
            type="text"
            placeholder="Username"
            value={username}
            onChange={(e) => setUsername(e.target.value)}
            required
        />
        <input
            type="password"
            placeholder="Password"
            value={password}
            onChange={(e) => setPassword(e.target.value)}
            required
        />
        <button type="submit">{isRegistering ? 'Register' :
        'Login'}</button>
        <button type="button" onClick={() =>
        setIsRegistering(!isRegistering)}>
            Switch to {isRegistering ? 'Login' : 'Register'}
        </button>
    </form>
  );
};

export default AuthForm;
```

Integrating the Authentication Form into the App

Update App.js to include the AuthForm component and manage authentication state:

```
javascript
Copy code
import React, { useState } from 'react';
import TodoList from './TodoList';
import AuthForm from './AuthForm';
```

```
function App() {
    const [token, setToken] = useState(null);

    return (
        <div className="App">
            {token ? (
                <TodoList />
            ) : (
                <AuthForm onAuth={setToken} />
            )}
        </div>
    );
}

export default App;
```

Testing User Authentication

1. Start your React application again using npm start.
2. Test the user registration and login functionality. Upon successful login, the Todo List should be accessible.

Step 5: Deployment and Finalization

Now that the full-stack Todo List application is complete, let's prepare for deployment.

Deploying the React Application

1. **Build the React Application**:

bash
Copy code

```
npm run build
```

1. **Upload the Build Directory to S3**:

- Create an S3 bucket to host your React application through the AWS Management Console.
- Enable static website hosting in the bucket settings.
- Upload the contents of the build directory to the S3 bucket.

Configuring CORS for API Gateway

To allow your front-end application to access the API, ensure that CORS is configured properly in API Gateway:

1. Go to the API Gateway console.
2. Select your API and navigate to the "Resources" section.
3. For each method (GET, POST, etc.), enable CORS and specify the allowed origins (e.g., your S3 bucket URL).

Testing the Deployed Application

1. Open the S3 bucket URL in your browser to access the React application.
2. Test the complete functionality, including user registration, login, and todo management.

Conclusion

In this chapter, we built a complete full-stack Todo List application using serverless architecture. By leveraging AWS Lambda, API Gateway, DynamoDB, and S3, we demonstrated how to create a scalable and cost-effective application without the need for managing infrastructure.

Key Takeaways

- **Serverless Benefits**: We explored the advantages of serverless computing, including scalability, cost efficiency, and reduced operational overhead.
- **Full-Stack Development**: The integration of front-end and back-end components in a serverless architecture showcased the flexibility and potential of serverless computing.
- **User Authentication**: Implementing user authentication with Amazon Cognito illustrated how to enhance application security and user management.
- **Deployment Best Practices**: We discussed best practices for deploying serverless applications, including the use of S3 for static hosting and configuring CORS for API Gateway.

As you continue your journey with serverless computing, consider the principles and techniques covered in this chapter to build robust and scalable applications. In the next chapter, we will summarize the key concepts from this book and discuss the future of serverless computing, highlighting emerging trends and directions.

Chapter 15: Conclusion and Future Directions in Serverless Computing

As we conclude this exploration of serverless computing, it's essential to reflect on the journey we've undertaken and the knowledge we've gained. Serverless architecture represents a paradigm shift in how we approach application development, deployment, and management. In this chapter, we will summarize the key insights from the book, discuss the broader implications of serverless computing, and explore future directions for this evolving technology.

Key Insights and Takeaways

1. Understanding Serverless Architecture

At its core, serverless architecture allows developers to build and deploy applications without worrying about the underlying infrastructure. This model abstracts away the complexities of server management, enabling teams to focus on writing code and delivering features. Key components of serverless architecture include:

- **Function as a Service (FaaS)**: The ability to deploy individual functions that respond to events, such as HTTP requests or changes in a database.

- **Managed Services**: Leveraging cloud provider services for storage, databases, and messaging without managing the infrastructure.
- **Event-Driven Design**: The architecture is fundamentally event-driven, allowing applications to react dynamically to user interactions or system events.

2. The Benefits of Serverless Computing

Serverless computing offers several compelling advantages, making it an attractive choice for organizations:

- **Scalability**: Serverless applications can automatically scale based on demand, ensuring that resources are used efficiently.
- **Cost Efficiency**: With a pay-as-you-go pricing model, organizations only pay for the resources they consume during function execution.
- **Faster Time to Market**: By removing the need to manage infrastructure, teams can focus on building features and accelerating their development cycles.
- **Reduced Operational Overhead**: The cloud provider manages infrastructure, allowing teams to concentrate on innovation and development.

3. Designing Effective Serverless Applications

To maximize the benefits of serverless computing, organizations must follow best practices in application design:

- **Microservices Architecture**: Breaking applications into smaller, independent services enhances maintainability and scalability.
- **Event-Driven Workflows**: Implementing event-driven architectures allows applications to respond dynamically to events and user interactions.
- **API Gateway Integration**: Using API Gateway as the entry point for serverless applications provides security, monitoring, and traffic

management.

4. Performance Optimization Strategies

Optimizing serverless applications for performance is crucial for delivering a responsive user experience. Key strategies include:

- **Reducing Cold Start Latency**: Implementing techniques such as provisioned concurrency, optimizing function sizes, and choosing faster runtimes can mitigate cold start issues.
- **Efficient Resource Management**: Adjusting memory allocations and timeout settings based on application needs can enhance performance and reduce costs.
- **Minimizing External Calls**: Using batching, caching, and asynchronous processing to reduce latency from external service interactions.

5. Cost Management Practices

Managing costs effectively is vital for organizations utilizing serverless architectures. Key practices include:

- **Monitoring Usage and Costs**: Tools like AWS Cost Explorer and AWS Budgets help track spending and identify areas for cost savings.
- **Optimizing Lambda Execution**: Regularly reviewing memory settings and optimizing API Gateway configurations can help control costs while maintaining performance.

6. Security Considerations

Security is a critical concern in serverless applications, and organizations must implement robust security measures to protect their resources and data:

- **Authentication and Authorization**: Implementing proper mechanisms, such as AWS IAM and Amazon Cognito, ensures secure access to serverless functions and APIs.
- **Data Protection**: Encrypting sensitive data in transit and at rest helps maintain security and compliance with regulations.

7. The Importance of Monitoring and Observability

Effective monitoring and observability are essential for maintaining the health and performance of serverless applications:

- **Using AWS CloudWatch**: This service provides metrics and logs that enable organizations to monitor serverless functions and troubleshoot issues effectively.
- **Implementing Distributed Tracing**: Tools like AWS X-Ray allow for visibility into request flows and performance bottlenecks across distributed components.

8. CI/CD for Serverless Development

Integrating Continuous Integration and Continuous Deployment (CI/CD) practices into the development process is crucial for serverless applications:

- **Automating Testing and Deployment**: Incorporating automated testing and deployment into the workflow ensures that code changes are validated before reaching production.
- **Utilizing CI/CD Tools**: Leveraging tools like AWS CodePipeline and GitHub Actions simplifies the CI/CD process and enhances collaboration among teams.

9. Future Trends in Serverless Computing

As serverless computing continues to evolve, several trends are shaping its future:

- **Multi-Cloud Strategies**: Organizations are adopting multi-cloud approaches to avoid vendor lock-in and optimize costs.
- **Serverless Containerization**: The convergence of serverless computing and containerization offers flexibility and portability for application deployment.
- **Enhanced Security Measures**: The increasing reliance on serverless architectures necessitates robust security practices to protect sensitive data.
- **Advancements in Observability**: Continuous improvements in monitoring and observability tools will enable organizations to gain deeper insights into application performance.

Broader Implications of Serverless Computing

1. Democratization of Software Development

Serverless computing democratizes software development by lowering barriers to entry. Developers can build and deploy applications quickly without needing extensive infrastructure expertise. This trend empowers startups, small businesses, and individual developers to innovate and compete in the market.

2. Accelerating Digital Transformation

Organizations embracing serverless computing are accelerating their digital transformation efforts. The agility provided by serverless architectures enables companies to respond quickly to changing market demands, improve customer experiences, and drive innovation.

3. Shifting the Focus to Business Logic

By abstracting away infrastructure concerns, serverless computing allows developers to focus on business logic rather than operational overhead. This shift enables teams to create applications that align more closely with business objectives.

4. Environmental Impact

The serverless model can contribute to a reduced carbon footprint by optimizing resource utilization and minimizing energy consumption. By leveraging shared infrastructure and efficient scaling, serverless architectures can lead to more sustainable software development practices.

Preparing for the Future of Serverless Computing

As organizations look to harness the power of serverless computing, they should take proactive steps to prepare for the future:

1. Invest in Training and Skill Development

Organizations should prioritize training and skill development for their teams to ensure they are equipped to leverage serverless technologies effectively. This includes fostering a culture of continuous learning and encouraging participation in relevant workshops, conferences, and certification programs.

2. Embrace a DevOps Culture

Adopting a DevOps culture can enhance collaboration between development and operations teams, streamlining the serverless development lifecycle. Encouraging cross-functional teams to work together can lead to better outcomes and improved software quality.

3. Experiment and Innovate

Encouraging experimentation and innovation within the organization can lead to new ideas and solutions. Provide teams with the freedom to explore new serverless tools, architectures, and patterns to identify opportunities for improvement.

4. Monitor Industry Trends

Staying informed about industry trends and advancements in serverless computing will help organizations adapt to changes and leverage new technologies effectively. Regularly engage with the developer community, attend conferences, and subscribe to industry publications to stay updated.

5. Foster a Customer-Centric Approach

As organizations build serverless applications, it's essential to prioritize user needs and experiences. Implement feedback loops to gather insights from users and iterate on applications to enhance their usability and value.

Final Thoughts

The journey through serverless computing has illuminated the vast potential of this architecture to transform how applications are built and managed. By embracing serverless technologies, organizations can achieve greater agility, scalability, and cost efficiency while focusing on delivering value to their users.

As the landscape of cloud computing continues to evolve, serverless architecture will play an increasingly critical role in shaping the future of application development. Organizations that embrace this paradigm and remain adaptable to emerging trends will position themselves for success in an ever-changing digital world.

Conclusion: Embracing the Future of Serverless Computing

T he evolution of serverless computing marks a significant shift in how we approach application development and deployment. By allowing developers to focus on code and innovation without the burden of managing infrastructure, serverless architectures have redefined the software development landscape. This chapter summarizes the key insights gained throughout the book and provides a forward-looking perspective on the future of serverless computing.

Reflecting on the Key Takeaways

Throughout this book, we have explored various aspects of serverless computing, from foundational concepts to advanced design patterns. Here are some key takeaways:

1. The Power of Serverless Architecture

Serverless architecture allows organizations to build scalable, flexible, and cost-effective applications. By decoupling the application code from infrastructure concerns, teams can deploy code quickly and respond to changing business requirements. The event-driven model inherent in serverless computing enables applications to react dynamically to user actions and system events, enhancing overall responsiveness.

2. Leveraging Managed Services

Serverless architectures are built on a foundation of managed services offered by cloud providers. These services—ranging from databases and storage to messaging and authentication—enable developers to create robust applications without having to manage the underlying infrastructure. This approach allows teams to focus on building features that deliver value to users rather than getting bogged down in operational tasks.

3. The Benefits of Scalability and Cost Efficiency

One of the most compelling advantages of serverless computing is its ability to scale automatically based on demand. This elasticity ensures that applications can handle traffic spikes without requiring manual intervention. Additionally, the pay-as-you-go pricing model associated with serverless computing allows organizations to optimize costs by paying only for the resources consumed during function execution.

4. Importance of Performance Optimization

Performance is a critical factor in the success of serverless applications. As organizations increasingly rely on serverless architectures, understanding and implementing performance optimization strategies becomes essential. Techniques such as reducing cold start latency, optimizing memory settings, and minimizing external calls can significantly enhance the user experience and ensure applications run efficiently.

5. Navigating Security Considerations

Security is a paramount concern in serverless computing. As organizations adopt serverless architectures, they must implement robust security measures to protect their applications and user data. This includes establishing proper authentication and authorization mechanisms, encrypting sensitive information, and regularly reviewing security practices to mitigate potential vulnerabilities.

6. The Need for Monitoring and Observability

Effective monitoring and observability are crucial for maintaining the health and performance of serverless applications. Tools like AWS CloudWatch and AWS X-Ray provide valuable insights into application behavior, enabling teams to identify issues, troubleshoot problems, and optimize performance. Establishing a culture of monitoring ensures that teams can proactively address potential bottlenecks and maintain application reliability.

7. The Role of CI/CD in Development

Continuous Integration and Continuous Deployment (CI/CD) practices are essential for streamlining the development process in serverless applications. By automating testing and deployment, organizations can enhance collaboration, reduce manual errors, and accelerate the release of new features. Implementing a robust CI/CD pipeline enables teams to deliver high-quality software consistently.

8. Embracing Future Trends

The serverless landscape is continually evolving, with emerging trends such as multi-cloud strategies, serverless containerization, and advancements in observability. Organizations must stay informed about these trends and adapt their strategies accordingly to leverage the full potential of serverless computing.

Looking Ahead: The Future of Serverless Computing

As we gaze into the future of serverless computing, several key developments are poised to shape its evolution:

1. Broader Adoption Across Industries

Serverless computing is gaining traction across various industries, from finance and healthcare to entertainment and retail. As organizations recognize the benefits of serverless architectures, we can expect increased adoption and innovation in this space. More companies will leverage serverless technologies to build agile applications that respond to user needs quickly.

2. Enhanced Integration with AI and Machine Learning

The convergence of serverless computing with artificial intelligence (AI) and machine learning (ML) is an exciting frontier. Serverless architectures can streamline the deployment of ML models, allowing organizations to process large volumes of data and make predictions without managing complex infrastructure. As AI and ML continue to advance, serverless computing will play a critical role in enabling real-time data processing and decision-making.

3. Evolving Security Practices

As serverless computing becomes more mainstream, security practices will evolve to address new challenges. Organizations will adopt advanced security frameworks and tools to protect their serverless applications from potential threats. Automated security testing and continuous monitoring will become standard practices to ensure robust security postures.

4. Greater Focus on Developer Experience

As serverless computing matures, there will be an increasing emphasis on improving the developer experience. Tools and frameworks will continue to evolve, simplifying the process of building, deploying, and managing serverless applications. This will empower developers to innovate faster and focus on creating high-quality software.

5. Enhanced Community and Ecosystem

The serverless community is vibrant and growing, with a wealth of resources, tools, and best practices being shared regularly. As more organizations adopt serverless architectures, we can expect an expansion of the ecosystem, including new libraries, frameworks, and tools that simplify development and enhance functionality.

6. Ongoing Research and Development

The future of serverless computing will be driven by ongoing research and development efforts. Cloud providers and technology companies will invest in developing new features and capabilities, enabling organizations to build even more powerful and efficient serverless applications. Innovations in areas such as event-driven architectures, managed services, and observability tools will continue to shape the serverless landscape.

Final Thoughts

The journey through serverless computing has highlighted its transformative potential and the opportunities it presents for organizations seeking to innovate and thrive in a digital-first world. By embracing serverless architectures, organizations can achieve greater agility, scalability, and cost efficiency, allowing them to focus on delivering value to their users.

As you move forward in your serverless journey, remember the key principles and best practices outlined in this book. Stay informed about emerging trends, continually optimize your applications, and foster a culture of innovation within your organization. By doing so, you will be well-equipped to navigate the future of serverless computing and unlock its full potential.

Thank you for joining this exploration of serverless computing. I hope you found it insightful and inspiring as you embark on your own serverless journey. The possibilities are limitless, and the future of serverless computing is bright.

www.ingramcontent.com/pod-product-compliance
Lightning Source LLC
LaVergne TN
LVHW051332050326
832903LV00031B/3491